JUMPS'
API _

This collection of engaging and simple to use activities will jumpstart students' learning and help the busy teacher to reinvigorate their teaching through the use of mobile apps and activities that can be used in the classroom.

A wealth of practical activities and advice on how to incorporate over 40 lively and exciting apps into the classroom will enable teachers to deliver creative lessons. This essential guide focuses on a range of apps, including Skitch, QR codes, Comic Life, Do Ink Green Screen, Puppet Pals, Our Story and much more.

This book offers much needed guidance on creative ways to integrate apps within the National Curriculum and how they can be incorporated into the teaching of Key Stages 1 and 2. Enabling teachers to deliver effective and imaginative lessons through the use of apps and providing links to a wide range of online resources, it covers all core areas of the curriculum:

- English, Maths, Science, Modern Foreign Languages, ICT, History, Geography and PE.

Jumpstart! Apps is an essential classroom resource that will encourage creative and independent learning in children and is the perfect solution for helping teachers, teaching assistants and students integrate apps into their daily practice, make the most of technology at their disposal and deliver imaginative and effective lessons.

Natalia Kucirkova is Senior Lecturer in Childhood, Youth and Education Studies at Manchester Metropolitan University, UK.

Jon Audain is Senior Lecturer in ICT/Computing and Music for Primary ITE at The University of Winchester, UK and an Apple Distinguished Educator (ADE).

Liz Chamberlain is a Senior Lecturer in Education at The Open University, UK.

Jumpstart!

Jumpstart! Science Outdoors
Cross-curricular games and activities
for ages 5–12
Janet Barnett and Rosemary Feasey

Jumpstart! Grammar (2nd Edition)
Games and activities for ages 6–14
Pie Corbett and Julia Strong

Jumpstart! Talk for Learning
Games and activities for ages 7–12
John Foster and Lyn Dawes

Jumpstart! PSHE
Games and activities for ages 7–13
John Foster

Jumpstart! History
Engaging activities for ages 7–12
*Sarah Whitehouse and
Karen Vickers-Hulse*

Jumpstart! Geography
Engaging activities for ages 7–12
Sarah Whitehouse and Mark Jones

**Jumpstart! Thinking Skills and
Problem Solving**
Games and activities for ages 7–14
Steve Bowkett

Jumpstart! Maths (2nd Edition)
Maths activities and games for
ages 5–14
John Taylor

Jumpstart! Spanish and Italian
Engaging activities for ages 7–12
Catherine Watts and Hilary Phillips

Jumpstart! French and German
Engaging activities for ages 7–12
Catherine Watts and Hilary Phillips

Jumpstart! Drama
Games and activities for ages 5–11
*Teresa Cremin, Roger McDonald,
Emma Goff and Louise Blakemore*

Jumpstart! Science
Games and activities for ages 5–11
Rosemary Feasey

Jumpstart! Storymaking
Games and activities for ages 7–12
Pie Corbett

Jumpstart! Poetry
Games and activities for ages 7–12
Pie Corbett

Jumpstart! Creativity
Games and activities for ages 7–14
Steve Bowkett

Jumpstart! ICT
ICT activities and games for
ages 7–14
John Taylor

Jumpstart! Numeracy
Maths activities and games for
ages 5–14
John Taylor

Jumpstart! Literacy
Key Stage 2/3 literacy games
Pie Corbett

JUMPSTART!
APPS

CREATIVE LEARNING, IDEAS AND ACTIVITIES FOR AGES 7–11

Natalia Kucirkova, Jon Audain and Liz Chamberlain

Routledge
Taylor & Francis Group

LONDON AND NEW YORK

First published 2017
by Routledge
2 Park Square, Milton Park, Abingdon, Oxon OX14 4RN

and by Routledge
711 Third Avenue, New York, NY 10017

Routledge is an imprint of the Taylor & Francis Group, an informa business

British Library Cataloguing in Publication Data
A catalogue record for this book is available from the British Library

Library of Congress Cataloging in Publication Data
Names: Kucirkova, Natalia, author. | Audain, Jon author. |
Chamberlain, Liz, author.
Title: Jumpstart! apps : creative learning, ideas and activities for ages 7-11
/ Natalia Kucirkova, Jon Audain and Liz Chamberlain.
Description: Abingdon, Oxon ; New York, NY : Routledge, 2017.
Identifiers: LCCN 2016009831 | ISBN 9781138940154 (hardback) |
ISBN 9781138940161 (pbk.) | ISBN 9781315674452 (ebook)
Subjects: LCSH: Education, Elementary--Computer programs. |
Application software. | Computer-assisted instruction. | Internet in
education. | Education, Elementary--Activity programs--Great Britain.
Classification: LCC LB1028.68 .K83 2017 | DDC 372.0285--dc23
LC record available at https://lccn.loc.gov/2016009831

ISBN: 978-1-138-94015-4 (hbk)
ISBN: 978-1-138-94016-1 (pbk)
ISBN: 978-1-315-67445-2 (ebk)

Typeset in Palatino and Scala Sans
by Saxon Graphics Ltd, Derby

Contents

Introduction

Tablets and iPads are now a common occurrence in Western classrooms, meaning that new software programs, the so-called 'apps' provided by these resources, add to the teachers' repertoire of pedagogic strategies and offer further options for fun and creative activities in the classroom.

There are various ways to engage in creative teaching and there is currently a large volume of apps advertised to support creative teachers. The aim of this book is to add some clarity to the field by offering tested activities and recommended resources to teachers who wish to enhance their practice with new technologies in a creative and engaging way. We want to go beyond the use of tablets to simply access the web or regulate group work and outline activities that support children's creativity and creative learning. We draw on activities we observed to work in the classrooms we visited and the tips and ideas many teachers generously shared with us. We hope this book will interest teachers and those who work with 7–11-year-olds, and help them with some practical tips and techniques for using apps to enrich their creative teaching practice.

The book is divided into 16 chapters. The first two chapters specify what we mean by creativity and the main characteristics of tablets. Chapters 3–16 outline specific apps and activities these support, in relation to specific subjects and six creativity categories.

We focus on creative apps that are cross-curricular in use and their potential to support creative practice in Key Stage 2, that is teaching 7–11-year-olds. We present Android and Apple apps, which are free as well as paid (we specify in brackets which is which). While Apple apps work on iPads, iPods and iPhones, Android apps work on Android tablets and smartphones developed by Acer, Motorola, Hudl, HTC, Samsung or Microsoft.

In our selection of activities, we were guided by the following three principles:

- to provide teachers with adequate guidance (how do the apps work, how might you adopt the activities, which apps are available for Android and iPads);
- to ensure that teachers are provided with activities that are easy to be integrated within existing practice;
- to provide instructional methodology (creative learning).

In defining creative ways of using apps to support the curriculum, we adopted the framework of *possibility thinking* which defines creative learning as transformation from what is to what might be. We were particularly interested in the power of possibility thinking to stimulate creative thinking in lower and upper Key Stage 2.

CHAPTER 1
Tablets and iPads

There are various kinds of technologies that might provide the resources necessary for creative activities. This book is concerned with tablets, sometimes called tablet computers. Tablets made by Apple are called iPads and represent the higher end of quality in the tablet market. Google Android tablets are very similar in design and functionality to iPads. In the UK, there are also cheaper alternatives sold by major supermarkets, similar in design to digital book readers. For ease of nomenclature, we will refer to both Android and Apple tablets as 'tablets' in this book. However, when describing individual apps, we will specify whether these are available for Android (or Google) tablets or iPads.

Tablets are more affordable than other screen-based technologies used in the school (e.g., interactive whiteboards) and are often available not only in schools but also in children's homes. There is thus a unique opportunity with tablets to extend learning in one environment to the other one and to bridge the home–school divide. In comparison to previous technologies, a distinct advantage of iPads for schools is that they are lightweight and portable. This means that they can be taken for school trips or used outside the classroom and, unlike desktop PCs, can be used to capture the dynamics of the learning experience as they happen in various locations.

Tablets are not only lighter, but also smaller and thinner than traditional laptops, and children can read text or study images on them as easily as they would with a normal-size book.

The touchscreen of tablets is another important usability feature, allowing quick and easy manipulation, even for children with limited dexterity. Tablets do not require separate input devices like computers (e.g., keyboards and mice), but fuse several technologies into one device: there is an inbuilt camera, microphone and keyboard, facilitating simultaneous activities in one location. The device is flexible enough to accommodate texts and images in various formats (for example, doc, docx and pdf for text) and there are several customisation options for reading the text on screen (e.g., possibility to enlarge the font, change background colour of the text).

Also, tablets come with a simple user interface: most navigation is icon-based, and there is only one main button, the so-called 'Home' button. Such an ergonomic design means that even very young children or children with very limited IT skills can proficiently navigate functions which before used to be integral to gadgets only available for older children (e.g., cameras or typewriters).

Another beneficial feature of tablets is that they can accommodate a large number of software programs, the so-called apps. Users can download apps for iPads from the App store and for all other tablets from the Googlemarket store. As of April 2015, there are more than a million apps in the iTunes store available for iPads and out of these, there are about 80 000 apps marketed as educational. There is a similar quantity of apps available for Android tablets. Given the large numbers, any topic covered in the elementary curriculum could potentially be supported by an educational app (Vaala, Ly & Levine, 2015) and several skills, preferences and needs can be catered for. As Sarah, a Year 6 student, said: 'I really enjoy the iBooks on the tablet because you can find any book; whereas in our library, there isn't as much variety and choices' (Ciampa, 2014, p. 91).

However, the large quantity of apps also implies that the quality of individual programs varies widely, and it is often difficult to find an app which would suit a particular teaching activity. In selecting the appropriate app, teachers can rely on other teachers' review sites (e.g., www.teacherswithapps.com; www.educationappreviews.com) or reviews put together by independent bodies, for example The Children's Technology Review (www.childrenstech.com).

When teachers choose apps independently, there are some rules of thumb they can follow. For instance, a well-designed app allows children to progress from novice to mastery for a range of skills, building on their motivations and interests. According to Hirsh-Pasek et al. (2015), educational apps are those which promote active, engaged, meaningful and socially interactive learning. Good apps are those which not only motivate but also extend children's learning, offering open-ended outcomes and incremental progress. In relation to reading for pleasure and supporting effective literacy engagement with digital books, Kucirkova, Littleton and Cremin (2016) outline six facets of reader engagement: affective, creative, interactive, shared, sustained and personalised reading engagements.

In practice, the characteristics of an app dovetail with those of the tablets, jointly supporting an activity. For example, creating digital multimodal stories with iPads is possible thanks to the features inbuilt in the hardware (microphone, front and back-facing digital camera, wifi networking capability) and apps allowing children to put their audio-visual contents together and share in one package with their friends online (e.g., the Our Story or Book Creator apps).

Balanced against these benefits, there are also limitations to the usefulness of tablets in classrooms. Two of the most significant hurdles preventing tablets' use in classrooms are the tablets' cost and teachers' confidence with technology. While tablets bring a lot of potential for reduction in costs associated with printing, storage and distribution of books and textual material, there is an initial investment. Different schools have used different strategies to purchase tablets, including the BYOD (Bring Your Own Device) model, subscription schemes or acquiring funds through parents' donations.

So that tablets are effectively used in classrooms, there needs to be ICT support in the school and some accompanying material for effective educational deployment of the devices. As with any technology or new resources more generally, there is a need for teacher training and professional development specifically tailored to the school's needs. It is also important that teachers are given extra time to identify the relevant apps that can support their lesson aims and objectives. It goes without saying that using tablets in a school efficiently also requires a robust wifi and broadband connectivity and funds necessary for tablet accessories (such as protective covers, cases, keyboards, headphones or chargers). It is beyond the scope of this book to outline these elements in more detail, but we highlight their importance before teachers embark on a creative journey of tablet use in their individual classrooms.

Different teachers use tablets in different ways, but typically, tablets work best when teachers identify a clear purpose of their use for a given activity. The context and content of the learning activity matter (Guernsey, 2012). Teachers need to think about how the activity fits their learning goals and how the tablet offers extra opportunities for specific children, including the highly talented as well as those with specific educational needs (Kucirkova, 2014).

While this book focuses on teachers' creative practices, it is often the case that children are app experts, with a lot of prior experience of apps' use or design. We therefore encourage teachers to support children in not only using but also co-creating apps and the learning content. Teachers can include children in their lesson plans and/or nominate some individuals to act as digital ambassadors. Digital ambassadors (sometimes called 'iChampions') can report about new apps, take care of the equipment or support children with less developed IT skills. Empowering children in managing the use of tablets in the classroom can be a very creative way of generating new ideas and igniting children's interest.

REFERENCES

Ciampa, K. (2014). Learning in a mobile age: an investigation of student motivation. *Journal of Computer Assisted Learning*, 30(1), 82–96.

Guernsey, L. (2012). *Screen Time: How Electronic Media – From Baby Videos to Educational Software – Affects Your Young Child.* Philadelphia: Basic Books.

Hirsh-Pasek, K., Zosh, J. M., Golinkoff, R. M., Gray, J. H., Robb, M. B. & Kaufman, J. (2015). Putting education in 'educational' apps: lessons from the science of learning. *Psychological Science in the Public Interest, 16*(1), 3–34.

Kucirkova, N. (2014). iPads in early education: separating assumptions and evidence. *Frontiers in Psychology, 5.* DOI:10.3389/fpsyg.2014.00715

Kucirkova, N., Littleton, K. & Cremin, T. (2016). Young children's reading for pleasure with digital books: six key facets of engagement. *Cambridge Journal of Education*, 1–18. DOI:10.1080/0305764X.2015.1118441

Vaala, S., Ly, A. & Levine, M. H. (2015). *Getting a Read on the App Stores: A Market Scan and Analysis of Children's Literacy Apps.* New York: The Joan Ganz Cooney Center at Sesame Workshop.

CHAPTER 2

Creativity

What do we mean by it?

Given that creativity is a multidimensional phenomenon and is often defined differently by different people, we need to specify what we mean by creative learning in this book.

When documenting and evaluating teachers' creative ways of using apps to support children's learning, we adopted the framework of *possibility thinking*. Possibility thinking foregrounds the notion of exploratory transitions from 'what is' to 'what might be' which enables children to engage in imagining worlds 'as if' they were in a different role (Craft, 2011b). Possibility thinking is core to creativity because it is the process through which questions are asked and problems are foregrounded (Jeffrey & Craft, 2004, p. 81). It involves a range of processes and children's behaviours, including question-posing, play, immersion, innovation, risk-taking, being imaginative, self-determination and intentionality. Possibility thinking is about 'problem solving as in a puzzle, finding alternative routes to a barrier, the posing of questions and the identification of problems and issues' (Jeffrey & Craft, 2004, p. 80).

How can teachers support possibility thinking? Building on Craft's (2001, 2011a, 2012) theoretical proposition, Grainger and Cremin (2001) outlined the ways in which adults (notably teachers) can facilitate and provide opportunities for children's possibility thinking in the classroom. In a series of studies, Cremin and colleagues (2006) observed and documented the practices of creative teachers in UK schools and identified three pedagogical strategies creative teachers employ to nurture possibility thinking in children's learning experiences:

1. the 'standing back' strategy in which the teachers discursively position themselves as agents of possibilities or 'what if' agents;
2. profiling learner agency, exemplified in action through the establishment of groups;
3. creating time and space in which learners' ideas were taken seriously and their independence was nurtured.

Creative teachers are thus those teachers who recognise the humanising potential of aesthetic, artistic and embodied knowledge and who are able to incorporate novel resources into their practice. They are not afraid to take risks and to go beyond performativity standards, ready to search for alternative learning spaces that acknowledge the fast pace of 21st century learning and the increasingly complex needs of young children.

In this book, we want to support such creative individuals and celebrate their practices by outlining strategies other teachers may wish to emulate in their own teaching contexts. It is our hope that the examples we present will be adopted by other teachers with an open mind and critical eye and that they will see them as suggestions to be appropriated and contextualised in their own settings. We encourage teachers to think about app-mediated creative activities as another way of enriching teachers' extant rich practices and as an opportunity to engage in collaboration with children and other teachers, who, as creative individuals, can all learn from each other. Although this book is focused on digital creative engagements, we wish to emphasise their synergistic relationship with non-digital resources and activities.

For a quick reference between possibility thinking, teacher practices and their presence within the individual activities in each chapter, we use a set of symbols and the following creativity categories:

Creativity category	Symbol
Play (includes playful engagements characterised by open-endedness & experimentation)	
Immersion (includes intense attention paid to a specific activity)	
Innovation (includes introducing new ideas and activities to a given context)	
Imagination (includes formation of new ideas, resourcefulness)	
Independence (includes self-determination and risk-taking)	
Mashup (includes combinations of creative activities within one)	

REFERENCES

Craft, A. (2001). Little 0 creativity. In A. Craft, B. Jeffrey & M. Leibling (Eds), *Creativity in Education*. London: Continuum (pp. 45–62).

Craft, A. (2011a). Approaches to creativity in education in the United Kingdom. In I. J. Sefton-Green, P. Thomson, K. Jones & L. Bresler (Eds), *The Routledge International Handbook of Creative Learning*. London: Routledge (pp. 129–139).

Craft, A. (2011b). *Creativity and Education Futures. Changing Childhood and Youth in a Digital Age*. Stoke-on-Trent: Trentham Books.

Craft, A. (2012). Childhood in a digital age: creative challenges for educational futures. *London Review of Education*, 10(2), 173–190.

Craft, A. & Jeffrey, B. (2008). Creativity and performativity in teaching and learning: tensions, dilemmas, constraints, accommodations and synthesis. *British Educational Research Journal*, 34(5), 577–584.

Cremin, T., Burnard, P. & Craft, A. (2006). Pedagogy and possibility thinking in the early years. *Thinking Skills and Creativity, 1*(2), 108–119.

Grainger, T. & Cremin, M. (2001). *Resourcing Classroom Drama, 5–8.* Sheffield: National Association for the Teaching of English (NATE).

Jeffrey, B. & Craft, A. (2004). Teaching creatively and teaching for creativity: distinctions and relationships. *Educational Studies, 30*(1), 77–87.

CHAPTER 3

Skitch

Editing and doodling on documents

Application

Skitch – a multi-purpose annotation tool

Subject possibilities

Science, Art, Geography, English

Category

- Android app – free
- Apple device (iPad/iPhone/iPod Touch) – free

WHAT THE APP DOES

Skitch is a camera-based application that allows the user to take a photograph or capture a screenshot before annotating and sending on. There are the familiar features, which include cropping images, adding colour, outlining shapes or creating text, all of which work using the touchscreen without the need for a stylus. Within the classroom the application might be used to create collaborative documents, make notes directly onto a piece of research or provide feedback for a classmate. In order to keep a copy of the image, it is important to save it before closing the application; the alternative is to attach a copy to an email and forward. Skitch can also be used in conjunction with other applications, for example, the collaging app PicCollage (see Chapter 3) or the QR code (see Chapter 4) reader scanner.

THE APP IN CONTEXT

The application has multiple uses across a range of subjects where note taking or annotations are the key focus skills. It is often said that a picture paints a thousand words; for example, in subjects like Science and Geography it is often easier to explain scientific knowledge or conceptual understanding through visual representation. Key Stage 1 children could use Skitch to capture images of a range of flowering plants before labelling their key structural features. The same activity could be applied to the identification and comparison between common animals, such as amphibians, reptiles, birds and mammals. In Key Stage 2, children can use Skitch to create and add their own questions or hypotheses about key scientific processes. Children could take a photograph of a plant and annotate using text and arrows how they think water is transported within plants.

TEACHERS' USE IN CLASS

The appeal of Skitch is that it captures a visual snapshot that can be shared immediately. Within shared reading or writing, teachers can demonstrate how an author has used description to create an image of a character and use Skitch to annotate the picture or text with the children's ideas. The activity can be showcased via the interactive whiteboard, and if the children have access to tablets, they can continue the activity independently. Skitch also has the potential to be a useful tool for providing formative feedback to children using the text annotations to suggest where improvements might be made in a piece of writing. The collaborative nature of the application would enable the children to respond to their teacher's suggestions through the creation of an annotated dialogue about the work.

ACTIVITIES

 The human body

Combine the use of research from books with exploring and naming parts of the body.

1. Take a photograph of the human body from a book.
2. At the top of the app are three buttons (undo, crop and clear annotations/rotate). Teach the children how to crop and image so they are just left with the clear outline of the human body without the surrounding writing. Save the image to the camera roll.
3. Ask the children to work in pairs and to photograph the clothed parts of their body. Then ask the children to use the pen tools to trace over the bones and joints so they can see the parts of the body over their own.
4. Label the parts of the body part using the books. Select the arrow tool to highlight different parts and then use the text tool to insert a label of the part.
5. As an extension task, ask the children to explain using the text tool what the body part does.

 Finding out more about your new class on transition day

1. Use the camera and ask each group to take a photograph of the whole group. Ensure there is enough room to be able to write information around the group photograph.
2. Ask the groups to work together and find out facts about each other.
3. Use the text tool located on the right-hand side of the screen. Press on the screen to write your text. On the left-hand side is a coloured dot. Press on this to change the colour of the text and also the size. Text can be moved to a different location by dragging the text box as well as resizing it by dragging the bottom right-hand corner of the box.

To save or export your work

1. Click on the Share icon (the box with the arrow).
2. Scroll across to either Save or Share tabs.
3. Under the Save menu, the annotated photograph can be placed directly into the camera roll or copied to the clipboard so it is then able to be pasted into another app. Alternatively, clicking the More icon will open up a dialogue box where you can then export the image into different apps installed on your device.
4. The Share tab will allow you to share through social media, such as Twitter, if the school has an account, or open up the photograph in another app.

Writing and editing work

1. Take a photograph of a piece of work.
2. Choose whether to focus on a section of writing or the overall text. Place the document in a shared area the children can access on their iPad (such as Dropbox) or email the photo to the children's iPads.

1. Use the Dropbox app and upload the photograph of the work.
2. Once uploaded, click the 'Share Link' box to get a shared link.
3. Copy this link by pressing on the link, selecting the entire link and then pressing 'Copy'.
4. Next, load the QR Code Reader app.
5. Create a new QR code for a website (see Chapter 4) and then paste the Dropbox link in and create the code.
6. This will enable you to display the code on the interactive whiteboard for the children to scan or print it out in the form of a physical code.
7. The children then scan the code to access the image of the piece of work.
8. As soon as the image comes up, encourage the children to press the 'Share' button and then to open the image in another app.
9. Next, select the Skitch app and the photograph will load.

3. Edit the work using the emoticons, underlining key points of style. You may select a small number of emoticons for the children to use, for example, smiley face means that children think the sentence is particularly strong instead of just liking a point. Press once to move the emoticon around if it has been placed in the incorrect position.
4. Press the 'Add' icon to add an arrow. Draw on the image to point to a specific point worth noting.
5. A text entry can also be entered so a comment can be written. Long sentences will need the user to resize the text.

⌕ Spot the difference

Ensure that the PicCollage and Skitch apps are both loaded on to the device.

Making a PicCollage

1. When you first load the app it will ask to access your photo roll. Ensure that you say yes to the request so you can insert the photographs you have taken into the collage.
2. Tap on a number of photographs you would like to make a collage out of and then touch the tick.
3. A default template will load straight away, although there are different options (you can switch the design by clicking the template design button in the bottom left-hand corner).
4. The finished design can then be shared by clicking the Share button and then saved to the camera roll.

---

1. Once the image has been saved to the camera roll, combine the two apps together.
2. Ask the children to use the camera to take a photograph of two different locations around the school grounds which show where their two favourite places are.
3. Use PicCollage to place the images side by side so it can compare the different settings.
4. Ask the children to create their collage and then export the finished collage to the camera roll.

5. Then reimport the collage into Skitch and ask the children to use the text tool to describe the features of their two favourite places.

Alternatively, here are some additional activities:

- Use Safari to find two contrasting photographs of geographic localities. When you have located two images, hold your finger on the image and a menu will come up to save the image to the camera roll. Create the collage and then use the text tool to describe how the two locations are different.
- Using objects, set up a scene of objects and take a photograph. Then remove a couple of the objects and retake the photograph. The children then need to circle the objects that are missing.

☁ Tell me a story

1. Ask the children to draw, create or locate a royalty-free image from the internet of a background scene.
2. Find a background for each of the different parts of a story (beginning, middle, end, complication, climax, conclusion) and then save these images to the camera roll.
3. Insert each image in turn into Skitch and then, using the text tool, encourage children to tell a story.
4. Place the text at the bottom of the screen, so the children have created a picture book.

This activity can also be used to create a social story to support children's emotional health and wellbeing in order to describe how a person may be feeling.

It's on the map

1. Use the free ordnance survey maps website (www.ordnance survey.co.uk/osmaps) to locate a map of the area. Alternatively, locate a map using Google Maps (www.google.co.uk/maps).
2. Take a screenshot of the map.

Screenshot the iPad screen

1. Hold down the on/off switch at the top of the iPad.
2. Press the round 'Home' button which will take a screenshot of the image that is on the screen. You do not need to hold it for too long. If your sound is active, you will hear the camera click and you will see the screen flash as the camera takes the image.
3. The screenshot will then be placed in the camera roll as an image for you to edit or insert into another application on the device.

---

3. Insert a map and use the tools (text, pen, shapes) to locate different geographical features children know about around the area. These could be landmarks, places that attract people, or places that nurture the environment.

Digital citizenship profiles

1. Explain to the children that we sometimes share too much information on the internet and that we can do this without realising.
2. Create a fictitious profile in a Word document by inserting information that may be considered to be over-sharing or too much information or that reveals information that should be kept private and not published on the internet such as made-up credit card details, passport numbers, or the security code to the ATM machine for your bank card.
3. Another site to use would also be Fakebook (www.classtools. net/FB/home-page) by Classtools, which enables you to create a fake Facebook profile, write posts and upload photographs.

4. Either save the information as a PDF document which will be in the drop down Save menu when you save a Word document or save as an image. Ensure that the information can be read clearly, so the children will be able to see the detail.

5. Place the images into a Dropbox account and provide a link to the children (see 'Writing and editing work' section for further guidance). If you saved the profile in a PDF format, then load the document on your iPad and screenshot the page so that it will be in the format of an image.

6. Ask the children to import the image(s) into Skitch.

7. Using the Pixelate tool, the children have to obscure sensitive information or information they think should not be on the form.

8. Use this activity as a discussion in terms of e-safety and their wider digital citizenship role. Does this create a better digital profile and leave a more acceptable digital footprint?

🔍 Art portraits

1. Use the camera tool and ask the children to take a selfie or alternatively work with a partner to take a photograph of their head and shoulders.

2. Import the image into Skitch.

3. Use the pen tool to support the drawing of portraits.

4. Ask the children to use the pen tool within Skitch to draw around their eyes, allowing them to better understand the actual shape they need to reproduce when creating the self-portrait on paper.

If you are able to source them, a stylus with a rubbery end that can be placed directly onto a normal pencil allows the children to draw directly onto the tablet but with the performance of a traditional pencil (see this website for more details: www.sensubrush.com/product/buddy-stylus).

OTHER APPS

PicCollage
QR Code Reader Scanner

CHAPTER 4

QR codes

Accessing and creating information points

Application

QR Code Reader – a scannable barcode containing information about the item it is attached to

Subject possibilities

History, Geography, English

Category

- Android app – free
- Apple device (iPad/iPhone/iPod Touch) – free

WHAT THE APP DOES

QR codes, or Quick Response codes, are a familiar feature when shopping, parking the car, or visiting a museum and can sometimes be found on clothing. Wherever information can be shared, a QR code can be used; the aim is to communicate complex ideas through a 2-D barcode, similar to the codes found on any household item you scan when doing self-service shopping. In a school setting, teachers can use a QR code to provide additional instructions or resources next to wall displays, as an interactive way of communicating with parents or as a new learning technology.

To create a QR code

1. Open the app and press on the '+' sign to create a new code.
2. Select a website and enter the URL of the website if known.
3. If the website is not known, then find the website on the mobile internet browser and select the website address. Once selected, copy the website address.
4. Then return to the app, create a new website QR code and paste in the weblink.

THE APP IN CONTEXT

In order to decipher a QR code, you need a code reader in the form of a handheld device, for example a smartphone or a tablet. So whilst not an application in the traditional sense, the ability to interpret and create codes allows children the opportunity to prepare and present material in a concise yet creative way. Museums and outdoor attractions have led the way in the imaginative use of QR codes, and you may have visited a nature reserve or your local gallery and been challenged to find things out or to follow an information trail. In History lessons, KS1 children can create a chronological framework of their school's history by using codes to explain the similarities and differences across the key features of the buildings. In KS2, a topic on the Vikings and Anglo-Saxons could lead to children working to create a group poster with additional information provided in the form of a video or quiz but presented as a QR code. Having learnt how to write and read a code, children can transfer these skills to instruction writing in Geography and responding to writing feedback in English.

TEACHERS' USE IN CLASS

QR codes are a useful aide-memoire for children and as such are invaluable aids for teachers. Instead of repeating key information, for example what PE kit is needed for which day, or key calendar events, QR codes can be displayed in the classroom. Parents and children can access the information at any time, which is helpful in promoting autonomy even in younger children. Key classroom information can also be provided for parents, and a rolling programme of QR codes can support parents in helping their children's learning at home. This might be through top tips for reading, sharing complex mathematical investigations or by providing a more interactive way of setting homework. The personalised nature of a QR code also makes it a useful tool for differentiation, for setting editing challenges prior to completion of work, or for simply feeding back to children about next steps.

ACTIVITIES

 Interactive classroom displays

Create an interactive display by adding a QR code to children's work; the link might provide more information, add a visual element or even have a film of the children talking about their work on display.

1. In the menu of the QR Code Reader app, press the three horizontal lines to reveal the app's menu.
2. Press the 'Creator' tab and then tap the plus button to add a new QR code.
3. Choose either a URL, YouTube or Notes link.

For a weblink (follow steps 1 and 3 and then go to step 4)

4. Tap the URL link and enter the website address (URL) for a website you wish to use on your display.
5. To copy a weblink from a website, browse for the site using the web browser and then highlight the web address by pressing the website link and then select all the address. Press 'Cut' or 'Copy', which will then store it in the computer's memory.
6. Return to the QR Reader app and paste it in the URL box that should still be open.

For a YouTube clip (follow steps 1 and 3 and then jump to step 7)

7. Go to YouTube, locate the video and then copy the website address (URL) for a video clip you wish to use on your display.
8. Highlight the web address by pressing the website link and then select all the address. Press 'Cut' or 'Copy', which will then store it in the computer's memory.
9. Return to the QR Reader app and paste it in the URL box, which should still be open.

For text (follow steps 1 and 3 and then jump to step 10)

10. Insert some text of your choice into the box by pressing and typing.

QR code topic map

This activity enables children and teachers to collate numerous links to websites and present these all on one page. Create a QR code History topic map detailing the significant turning point in British history at the time of the Battle of Britain in 1940.

Making the map:

1. Search the internet for a topic-related image; this image will be the backdrop of your QR topic map. Ensure the image is not cluttered so the QR code can be placed appropriately on the image.
2. Save this map to the camera roll (see Chapter 6).
3. Create ten QR codes for different websites connected to the topic.
4. Save these to the camera roll.
5. To assimilate your map you will need an app that will provide you with a blank template to use (PowerPoint, Keynote, Book Creator).
6. Insert the topic background you found.
7. Insert each of the QR codes in turn and arrange on the map.
8. Print out the finished map and attach to the wall or stick into the children's books.

How to use the map:
- Create the QR map at the beginning of the topic. Use the map as a knowledge navigation tool so that the children can cross-reference their current familiarity with the topic.
- Use the map during the topic as a learning map, with some suggested routes into the next phase of learning. Give children an element of choice as to what they study next.
- At the end of the topic, use the map to support summative assessment by asking the children to reflect on what they know about the topic.

Creating a QR code poster

Use this activity to help your new class at the beginning of the year to understand your classroom routines.

---

1. Create a QR code using the instructions in this chapter. When you create the code, press on the text next to the code and you will then be given a number of options. One of the options is the ability to be able to share your QR code using email; this sends the QR code as an image, which you can then insert into a document.
2. Insert the QR code and then type your instructions for the children to follow after they have scanned the code, or just provide a number or a heading so the children know they are in the correct place.

An interactive classroom tour

Create the QR codes using the same instructions as before; these might include:

✓ Mr Audain really likes it when you hang up your coats and bags and your cloakroom is spotless at the end of the day. Extra team points are awarded at the end of the day.
✓ Any notes, letters, money in an envelope or anything Mrs Chamberlain has to see, put them into this tray.
✓ On the wall I have placed a list of jobs we need people to do around the classroom. Take a look at the list of jobs and sign

up for a job you would like to help out with in the classroom. Thank you, Miss Kucirkova.

The children can start the school year with an interactive tour and scan the codes to find out more information about the classroom. You could also use the same principle to create a *'Don't forget'* display, by creating a tree with a QR code at the end of each branch.

 Instructions

Type instructions for your class to follow. Use them as a checklist so children can review and edit their work before they come to see you. For example: *'Don't forget to check your capital letters and full stops. Have you remembered to include an adjective and an adverb?'*

Other ideas might include:

✓ Create a set of instructions as a checklist for more complex activities, which will avoid you having to repeat instructions too many times.
✓ Provide a list of reading comprehension questions for the text you are reading.
✓ Copy and paste your class assembly script so that the children can learn their lines at home.
✓ If the children have their own personal devices, create a list of homework tasks and equipment they will need to prepare for the next day.
✓ You could also use the same method for explaining maths investigations or problem-solving activities without having to deliver (and repeat) lengthy or complex instructions.

Make a YouTube clip

1. To make YouTube videos, you need to sign up for a free YouTube account via a Google account. Select your option from Android, computer, mobile site or iOS. If you are using a computer, log in and click **Create Account** and you will see the option to **Upload**. On the right-hand side there is a short menu, which allows you to create videos using YouTube and upload them.

2. Click on the web cam capture and, providing your laptop has a web camera, you can record video footage of you explaining a task or showing the children what they need to do. *You may need to allow access to your camera first by ticking the* **Allow** *box.*

3. An alternative to using the web application is to use the YouTube capture app (https://itunes.apple.com/gb/app/youtube-capture/id576941441?mt=8) which works in exactly the same way.

Treasure hunt around the school

Draw or locate an outline map of your school that is clear enough for the children to follow. Place round sticker dots on the map to show where the children will find the QR codes. Display the map in the classroom and, at the beginning of the activity, ask the children to take a photograph of the map so they know the places they are looking for. The photograph provides a useful aide-memoire throughout the task.

Make a QR code poster for each of the stickered places with a QR code for either an activity or a task to complete. You might also record film footage of you introducing a new idea or film from the next location the children are seeking.

QR codes for assessing writing

Create a text-based QR code where you insert questions for the children to respond to before you mark their writing. Teach the children to find where the **history** tab is within the app. (When a QR code is scanned a record of it is kept in a history log.) To access the log, click on the three horizontal lines and select the history option. Remember to click on the horizontal lines again so that the grey menu at the side disappears.

Click on the code you want for further information about it or to load it up. Then look for the Share button (a square with a vertical arrow). Press the arrow and ask the children to share the QR code into the notes app by pressing the notes icon. As you load the notes app, you will see all the information listed there. The children can then type into the notes app and use your previously recorded questions as a framework for editing their work. When the children have finished, the notes can then be emailed to their teacher or they can keep their own copy as a record or they can email them ready for printing.

 ### QR codes prompts for improving writing
Use the same principle for creating a QR code poster but this time create laminated bookmark size versions, which can either be kept on the table for reference or stuck into the children's books.

For each bookmark, create guidance for the children to support a specific aspect of their learning. For example, if the QR code is a prompt to improve their writing, the bookmark could be: tips for writing; level descriptors; suggestions on how to improve first drafts; or could provide exemplars of what outstanding writing in the specific genre may look like.

 ### QR codes for providing feedback to pupils
Create a generic text-based QR code with a bank of positive learning behaviour statements and next step target statements. Personalise the statements by deleting those that are not applicable and by adding a personal comment specific to the child. Print out the QR codes on to stickers or paper that the children can stick into their books, or they could keep as a digital record on their iPad.

 ### QR codes to support differentiation
Create three QR codes for the children at three different attainment levels. Divide the children into groups according to their attainment level. Assign a colour to each group (for example, groups 1 and 3, your spellings are on the QR codes on the GREEN pieces of paper; group 2, your spellings are on the QR code on the YELLOW piece of paper).

Print out the individual QR codes and stick onto the different coloured pieces of paper. Ask the children to scan the QR to collect their spellings or extension tasks.

QR codes as communication for parents

Use QR codes to provide information to parents; stick the QR code poster on the window or door of the classroom and parents can scan the code as they are waiting to collect their children. Some ideas are listed below:

- Use a QR code to provide parents with a list of important classroom or year group dates so parents can scan the code and use the information as a checklist or as entries into their own diaries.
- Create a latest newsletter QR poster that just contains text information and place these around the school. Parents can then scan the code to receive the latest information, reducing the risk of lost letters.
- Create a poster linking to your latest class blog post, or linking to the school website.

QR codes to support home learning

Create small text-based QR codes with top tips for:

- Improving your child's reading.
- Making a comfortable reading environment at home.
- Recommended authors by age range or year group.
- Suggested questions to probe deeper understanding of text for home shared reading.

CHAPTER 5

Comic Life

Your learning in pictures

Application

Comic Life – a template-based application combining photographs and text

Subject possibilities

Geography, English

Category

- Apple device (iPad/iPhone) – paid
- Android app – not available, alternative Comic Strip It (Lite version) – free

---

WHAT THE APP DOES

The Comic Life application contains a series of templates which provide children with easy access to creating their own comics by combining photographs and text. As a paid app and one that is only available on iOS devices, it may currently have limited use in the classroom. However, there is a Lite version available in the form of Comic Strip It. It is included here because, as technology develops, there will be other applications that provide a similar platform and the ideas can be transferred.

Getting started with Comic Life

1. Click the page icon and a menu will appear with three headings – comic, template and layout.
2. The **comic** tab will allow you to add new pages to your comic. If the number of key points exceeds the number of boxes on the template, adding an extra page and then applying another layout can be useful. To delete a page whilst in comic mode, just tap the comic page and press on 'Delete'.
3. The **layout** tab will present you with a number of different comic layouts that you can apply to your selected page. Press on the layout and it will load on the screen for you.
4. If you wish to see the page you are working on, return to the top-right corner and click the page icon to the right of the plus button and click comic. The page with the tick in the bottom right-hand corner is the page you are currently working on.

THE APP IN CONTEXT

Presenting information in a series of comic strips either in a History lesson or when writing a story in English has been a popular strategy taken by many primary teachers. What Comic Life addresses is the familiar problem of children trying to include too much text in one cell, or realising too late that they have planned too few cells. To be able to storyboard effectively requires children to break down an idea into a series of steps; this may be in the form of key incidents in a story or recount, or through the presentation of historical information in a chronological timeline of events (see Chapter 6 concerning the app Our Story with more specific ideas about this). The application provides a useful framework to support the investigation process in subjects such as Geography, as it enables children to communicate their understanding of key concepts through creative explanations or to demonstrate of their understanding of collected data.

TEACHERS' USE IN CLASS

Comic Life also provides teachers with an original way of sharing information. In staff meetings, teachers can capture key events through a series of photographs that can then be matched to appropriate captions. This creative approach highlights the importance of capturing key information, such as next steps for staff, agreed approaches to marking work or points to remember for the week. It may also be an innovative way of communicating with parents instead of the more conventional paper-based newsletter.

ACTIVITIES

 ### Creating geographical factfiles

Top Trumps is an exciting way of sharing information and can be easily made for a topic so new knowledge can be learnt. Further details of how to play can be found at www.toptrumps.com/how-to-play-top-trumps.

Decide on a theme for the factfile (this example uses a geographical theme). Decide on the categories for the card (name, location, most interesting place to visit, etc.) and then determine further categories with numerical values attached to them (population, time it takes to fly there from the UK).

Begin a new comic and create a box for the image. Select the text box and enter the different categories, beginning a new text box each time. Once the first template is made, encourage the children to try to fit four or six cards to a page. Print out the cards and then cut out the cards ready to play the game.

 ### Going back in time

Comics are a great way of displaying time sequences and are a useful way of capturing historical events in a succinct and engaging way.

Ask the children to use the Notes app to jot down the key points they have found out through their research of a famous person in history. For example, KS2 children can research the lives of the six wives of Henry VIII, whilst in KS1 children can find out about the key facts of the plague or the Great Fire of London. Count how many key facts have been written down and load the Comic Life app; each fact will have its own cell in the app.

Styling the cells

1. At the bottom of the screen is a tray with different callout bubbles, text boxes, comic lettering and the ability to add a new photograph box to the page being worked on.

2. Ask the children to select one page. Explain that the boxes can be manipulated by tapping the box when the blue 'select' line and 'resize' handles appear.

3. By dragging the resize circles it is possible to fit the number of cells needed to include each of the key facts. The boxes can be styled by selecting a cell and clicking the brush, and proceeding along the tabs.

Ask the children to resize/drag onto the page the required number of boxes they need to illustrate the key points of their timeline. There are some extremely interesting effects that can be used such as the scroll effect that could be used to introduce a historical person or to provide introductory information to set the timeline in context.

Images can also be added to illustrate each of the key points in the historical timeline. Remember that a key feature of the app is that it combines both text and images to good effect.

Inserting images

1.	There are three ways to insert an image into the box when the picture icon (in the middle of the comic box) is pressed: by taking a **photo** on the iPad, accessing the **Photo Library** or adding a **web image**.

Taking a photo

1.	Press the camera option (the first time you select this option it may ask your permission to access your photographs. Press 'Allow' so the apps can see and use the images).
2.	Point the camera at an image the children wish to use. This may be from one of the school library books or a drawing or from physical objects. (You will need to check copyright and permissions when using images from the internet.)
3.	Press the shutter button and then 'Use Photo' once the image has been taken.

Inserting an image from the Photo Library

1.	Press the photo library option and the Photos pane will appear.
2.	Locate the photo from the correct folder. If the children have saved images from Safari or other mobile web browsers then they can also be inserted.
3.	The images can be rotated by tapping the image and using two fingers to turn it.

Web images

1.	Press the Web images option and then select Flickr.
2.	Search for an image and click to insert the image.
3.	When the image is inserted, the name and Flickr licence is also inserted. Use this opportunity (if this function is active) to teach the children about copyright and how we must acknowledge where photographs come from, unless we have taken the images ourselves.

4. When the text is selected, press the brush, which will allow for the writing in the box to be made smaller. Perhaps the name and licence can be copied into the same box as they are separated in two separate boxes.

Combine the images and text boxes to show the sequence of events. The finished comic can be shared by pressing the spanner icon and selecting the Share and Print option. This will present three options: 1) to print wirelessly if this option is available, 2) to send a copy using an email account or 3) to open the comic in another app.

⊗ Be an explorer

Using either real physical objects or images of objects, ask the children to photograph an artefact. This could also be paired with a visit arranged to a museum or through a practical classroom workshop.

Ask the children to take a photograph of their artefact or object before beginning a new blank comic. Insert an image box from the content tray and drag the edges of the image box to fill three-quarters of the screen and insert a text box.

Ask the children to describe their object and craft a short sentence with a focus on the key features. Click on the '+' button and select the second option which allows arrows to be placed around the image and can be combined with the label.

Continue adding the text boxes to describe when the object was discovered, where the object was discovered and what it would originally have been used for.

✎ Creating instructions

Load Comic Life and add a new comic by clicking '+' in the top left-hand corner. Scroll through the templates to find the 'How to' template category. Explain to the children that they are going to be creating an algorithm (i.e. step-by-step instructions) on how to make a jam sandwich.

Tell the children they will be adding the instructions later, but for now, you are going to make a jam sandwich in front of them. Ensure children have access to a mobile device and ask them to use the camera to take a photograph of each stage of the process. The photographs serve the purpose of an algorithm, i.e. a series of detailed, easy-to-follow instructions.

Make the jam sandwich in front of the children whilst they take the photographs using the camera app. Select the blue pre-made 'How to' guide. Insert the images and use these as a prompt for writing the instructions on how to make the sandwich.

New pages can be inserted and alternative templates can be applied by clicking the template option; double tapping and editing the information can customise any of the options, bubbles, numbers and boxes.

☁ Storytelling

Explore comics written for children. Mental Floss has an interesting article on comics for early readers (http://mentalfloss.com/article/62202/10-great-kids-comics-early-readers) which is worth exploring as is the work of Raymond Briggs (www.penguin.co.uk/authors/raymond-briggs/17111).

Ask the children to explore the comics and look at how the story has been created. Talk about the way the story has been storyboarded and how the text is easy to read. Begin a new comic, click the page icon in the top right-hand corner and select a layout.

Discuss ideas for a story outline (combine with English unit of work) and ask the children to choose a layout that will support the organisation of their own story. The children can either draw the pictures for their comic or select and fit appropriate images collected from other sources.

☼ Teaching onomatopoeic sound words

On a blank new comic, explore the concept of words that make sounds. Ask the children to click the 'Lettering' option in the content tray and spell out words that make a sound when they are pronounced.

Challenge the children to think about the way a word may look visually. For some words, the children may have to enter in the word letter by letter so they can apply their chosen effects.

Click on the word (or letter) and click the 'Lettering' option where the children can then change the font, spread, stagger and skew of the word.

By clicking the '+' option in the top right-hand corner and selecting the third option, the children can then embed stickers onto their comic. Many of these options have onomatopoeic elements. Although the words cannot be edited, they may be useful to support children who need inspiration.

Explaining new concepts or demonstrating what you know

Begin a new blank comic. Challenge the children to choose an area of the curriculum they need to explain to an unknown audience. For example, KS1 children could explain mathematics to an alien visitor, or older children could explain changes to technology to a time traveller from the Victorian era.

Drag a comic box to the middle of the page. In the middle of the box ask the children to place a picture of the chosen object/example/ product. Around the edge of the box, the children have to add text to explain or demonstrate the process from start to finish.

The same principle could be applied when creating handy how-to guides, revision guides or for children to demonstrate what they know about a completed project.

STAFF MEETING ROUND UP

Why not condense the main points from a staff meeting or INSET day in a handy one-page summary for absent staff and support staff?

During the meeting/training, take a photograph of the speaker or member of staff who is presenting the information. Set the Comic Life template by selecting the page icon in the top right-hand corner and press on 'Layout'.

Presenting the staff meeting notes in this way encourages a sense of succinctness about the main points from the training.

READ ALL ABOUT IT!

Begin a new comic by pressing the '+' in the top left-hand corner. Scroll down to the 'Education' section and locate the newspaper template and press on it to load a blank version of the template. Remember to select the page icon in the top right-hand corner and press the template button where you will also find a further three additional pages in the newspaper format. The information can be edited in the usual way.

CHAPTER 6

Personalising with the Our Story app

Application

Our Story

Subject possibilities

History, Science, Mathematics, Design Technology, Modern Foreign Languages

Category

- Apple device (iPad) – free
- Android app[1] – free

WHAT THE APP DOES

Our Story is a story-making app, similar to Book Creator in that users can create their own stories using pictures, text and audio recordings. Unlike Book Creator, the app also includes the possibility to create video-based stories and colour-coded templates for children's digital research projects. The user interface consists of a gallery of pictures and a filmstrip at the bottom, where pictures can be dragged down and arranged in a sequence (see figure below).

Creating a new story: the Create mode

Finished stories can be shared in their multimedia format (including all the videos, audio files and textual files) by choosing the Dropbox feature embedded within the app. If you wish to have a printed record of the texts and/or pictures, you can choose from three formats: A4, A5 or A6.

Choosing a print size of a finished story

THE APP IN CONTEXT

A key feature of Our Story is that it supports personalisation of multimedia content. The possibility to create texts, pictures and sounds is an important motivating factor for children who typically feel more motivated and interested in taking part in an activity which they can personalise. Personalised learning material is also more engaging and meaningful, enabling children to make a connection between their own lives and the educational content. Some research also shows that personalising teaching content supports children's retention and understanding of new learning content. So, whether you teach lower or upper Key Stage 2, consider spicing up your teaching with some fun digitally mediated personalisation.

ACTIVITIES

 **In the life of ...**

The primary History curriculum contains several opportunities for children to develop empathy skills and greater understanding of the lives of ordinary children, adults and families in various eras. You can ask children to imagine being a child during the Second World War or in the Victorian era or in Ancient Rome.

1. Download a few copyright- and royalty-free images from the internet, representing a different era.
2. Through AirDrop (see Chapter 15) or another file-sharing mechanism in your school, share these pictures with children's iPads/tablets.
3. Ask children to tap on the camera roll icon from within the Our Story app – this will populate their gallery of pictures within the app with your pictures.
4. Ask children to pretend to be a child in a given era and to select the right pictures representing that era. What would they eat, which objects would they use and what clothes would they wear?

5. Ask children to drag the relevant pictures down on the filmstrip and put them in a sequence.
6. Children can add their own texts and sounds to accompany each picture. Tap the image on the filmstrip; this will enlarge the picture to occupy the whole screen. Tap the white box to bring up a keyboard to type text or the microphone button to record an audio file.
7. Finished stories can be shared in the class as short dramatised scenes, with each child presenting their own story.

Recording sounds

There are no restrictions or templates in Our Story; you and the children can record any sounds they wish to accompany their stories or pictures. The length of a single recording isn't limited, so it can be a short sentence or a long narrative. However, the finished recording cannot be edited, so it might be best to make short recordings where you don't mind deleting the file and replacing it with another one.

Children can record their own voices but also the sound of various musical instruments, as well as sounds from the neighbourhood, from the nearby park, etc. Experimenting with the audio-recording quality is an important digital skill, making children aware of the various sounds – and silences – around them.

This activity could be also adapted for an English lesson, with children taking on the persona of their favourite writers or book characters. Follow a similar procedure and encourage children to narrate and/or write texts characterising the person they represent. This will make them feel more motivated to read about the character and explore various details in the character's biography, possibly recognising connections to their own lives.

⊗ Creating a local archive

Encourage children to explore their local history and become more aware of their local community by interviewing their neighbours and other residents. Children's historical awareness of their local area will be further promoted if the children are given access to local photo and recording archives. This activity may be especially suited for the Local and Community History Month (1–31 May) but can be used throughout the year.

1. Access the local archive (see the next box) and download a set of historic pictures and other relevant artefacts from a given historic period.
2. Ask the children to use their iPad cameras to take pictures of areas in the community/neighbourhood depicted in the historic pictures.
3. Ask the children to describe the key differences between then and now. Tap on the white box below each picture to add text.
4. Finished pictures with children's text can be printed by tapping the printer icon and selecting a format size. To adjust the font to the paper format (e.g., smaller font for smaller format), go to the app settings. Exit the app and tap on 'Settings'. Select Our Story and the font options can be chosen from there.

Accessing local archives

If you don't have the time or resources to visit your local library or council, local archives can be conveniently accessed online. For example, the Record Office holds archives about family history, house history and local studies of all areas in England and Wales. You need to type in a postcode to start the search: www.gov.uk/search-local-archives

The Discovery website of the National Archives (http://discovery.nationalarchives.gov.uk/) is the largest archive site, with more than 32 million descriptions of records, 2,500 archives and over 9 million downloadable records. The site also contains podcasts and videos and specifically designed lesson plans (www.nationalarchives.gov.uk/education/sessions-and-resources/?resource-type=lesson) which are mapped to KS2 curriculum and can be used as they are for History lessons or adapted for specific topics.

You can also encourage the children to interview their neighbours, elderly members of the community or other local residents about the places they photographed and make their archives audio-visual. To add an audio recording to a specific picture, you need to tap the microphone icon as soon as you start recording. Alternatively, you can use another audio-recording app and match the pictures and sounds later.

Audio-recording apps

There are several free audio recorder apps for Android tablets and iPads. Both have a simple user interface and can record and play back recorded sound. The apps use built-in tablet microphones so if you need to adjust the volume, remember to top up the volume of the tablet as well as that in the app.

The iPad microphone is located on the top of the iPad, to the middle of the back edge. You don't need to hold it close to the speaker's mouth but be careful in areas with a lot of background noise.

The location of tablet microphones varies, but they are usually along the bottom edge, and the volume control rocker is usually located on the upper right side of the tablet.

 Documenting how plants grow

Helping plants grow is an exciting way of teaching the basics of how to keep plants healthy and help them grow well. Ask the children to document in photographs the process of growing various vegetables and to include pictures of other relevant stages (e.g., decay, germination, seed dispersal). Depending on the season, they can also include how, for example, autumn leaves change colours or spring flowers shoot up. The final stage of the plant growth can be shared as a video, with the child narrating their strategy to ensure the plant has enough warmth and water. This video can be uploaded to the classroom's (or school's) Vimeo/YouTube account and shared as a QR code with parents and other children (see Chapter 4).

Individualised discovery

The BBC Bitesize website (www.bbc.co.uk/bitesize/ks2/science/ living_things/) contains many interactive games for Science. In classrooms with good wifi connection and several tablets, children can watch the videos and play the interactive games and progress through the different levels at their own pace. The activities teach children about plants and animal habitats but also the KS2 key topic: the human body (including circulation and locating body parts). You will need a set of headphones for each child/tablet to allow them to explore the site at their own pace.

 Digital food chains

The filmstrip feature of Our Story is ideal for customising the process and examples of food chains. Children can individualise the food chain by adding animals from familiar ecosystems (e.g., animals they saw in the school garden or on the school trip) or by adding their favourite animals.

1. Ask the children to upload to the tablet picture folder pictures from their local ecosystem, featuring the life processes and living things in the environment they are familiar with. The pictures can be downloaded from the internet or taken with the tablet camera.
2. Ask the children to go to the RSPCA website (www.rspca.org. uk/home) and add to the gallery pictures of endangered species. Encourage children to think about ways your school could be more animal-friendly.
3. Encourage children to create two sets of folders in their camera roll on the iPad: one which features producers and one with consumers.
4. Open the Our Story app and ask children to drag to the filmstrip animals illustrating a simple food chain (beginning with a producer, followed by an animal for which the previous animal represented food).

5. When finished, encourage children to explore animals and the food chains of different habitats (e.g., desert, polar, savannah, wetlands). Ask them to download some pictures of animals representing the various habitats and create folders in their camera rolls. These animals can then be used for new digital food chains created with the Our Story app.

Creating folders and sub-folders on tablets

You can group apps (app icons) or pictures (in the photo gallery) into folders and sub-folders on a tablet just like you would on a desktop PC. The procedure is the same for tablets and iPads.

1. Tap and hold one of the icons (or pictures) you wish to group into a folder.
2. Drag the selected icon (or picture) over the top of another icon (picture).
3. Release the selected icon/picture and a folder will be created containing both icons/pictures.

 Personalised dictionaries

Looking for a fun and memorable way to teach children new vocabulary? Whatever the MFL language, you can create customised or personalised dictionaries for the children or encourage them to create their own.

1. Decide on a list of up to ten new vocabulary items.
2. Ask children to look for objects representing these words in their surroundings and take a picture with the tablet camera.
3. Insert the pictures into the Our Story gallery (by tapping the camera roll icon).
4. Annotate each picture with the relevant word. You can switch the keyboard to a different language when needed (see Chapter 15 for details).
5. You can print the finished pictures with words as one-sided flashcards or you can keep them in the app and add sounds to each picture.

6. The sound could be simply exemplifying the correct pronunciation of the word or it could be an illustration of using the word in a sentence or context. Tap on the microphone icon next to the keyboard in Our Story and encourage children to add a recording according to their abilities.

📍 Create a history line

There are several downloadable timeline cards available on teacher resources websites (e.g., www.primaryresources.co.uk/history/history.htm) and with Our Story, you can ask the children to create their own, using their own pictures or drawings.

1. Ask the children to draw a picture representing a historic milestone (e.g., 'Romans invade Britain'; 'Great Fire of London').
2. Using the tablet camera, take a picture of this drawing, so that it can be used as a picture and inserted into the Our Story app from the tablet camera roll. Alternatively, you can scan the picture with a scanner and email it to yourself. Then you can download the picture from your email onto an iPad/tablet.
3. With various pictures created by the children representing various key historical events, you can create a digital history line which can be shared digitally and enriched with children's audio recordings. The original drawings can be used to decorate your classroom.

🔅 Ordering and sequencing

You will be familiar with the worksheets featuring caterpillars for children to write on sequences of numbers, fractions or decimals. With Our Story, you can create any sequence you like, personalise it with the children's favourite animal or character and let them complete the sequence digitally. For instance, children can be asked to order weights (e.g., put in the right order 4, 2, 12, 9 and 16 grams), or a random set of numbers within a range of 0–20 or positive and negative numbers. This activity is good for developing mathematical vocabulary and can be set as group work, with a group of 2–3 (4 maximum) children completing a sequence on one iPad/tablet.

1. Ask the children to decide which animal/creature will represent their group's sequence. Children can either draw this creature or download a picture from the internet or take a picture with the tablet camera.
2. Print the picture out and cut it into several pieces (depending on how long you want the overall sequence to be).
3. Take pictures of the individual pieces of the sequence (children can do this too).
4. Populate the Our Story gallery of pictures with the cut pictures and ask the children to assign a number (or decimal or fraction) to each, putting them in the right order on the filmstrip. Children will need to first drag the first piece of the sequence onto the filmstrip (e.g., a caterpillar's head), then tap on the picture to pull up the keyboard and then type in the right number. To switch on the numeric keyboard, tap on the numbers icon on the actual keyboard.
5. Finished sequences can be printed or shared between groups of children for collective feedback or emailed to you to check.

You can create a sense of competition by timing the construction of a sequence. There are several timer apps available for tablets.

Timers for tablets

There are several stylish paid apps for showing and recording time, but their free alternatives will definitely serve the purpose too.

The *Timer + app* works on Android and Apple devices and can be programmed to set multiple timers (up to 20) at once. You can time by the second, minute or hour, without the need to constantly check the app (it runs in the background while you use other apps): https://itunes.apple.com/us/app/timer+/id391564049?mt=8

For a visually more appealing timer, you can use the *Giant Timer app* which is free and features big clear digits and effective sounds and pre-recorded messages (e.g., 'Done!') as an alarm: https://itunes.apple.com/us/app/giant-timer/id366679407?mt=8

Sand Timer is a digital equivalent to a sand timer and is free for both Android and iPad devices: https://itunes.apple.com/us/app/best-sand-timer/id501940934?mt=8

👤 Getting healthy with a digital diary

1. Ask the children to take pictures of the foods they eat for breakfast. They can use a standard digital camera or borrow a smartphone from their parents to do so.
2. Ask the children to email the picture to your email account and upload them to the students' iPads (using the standard photo-sharing mechanism enabled by the tablet).
3. In small groups, ask the children to rank their foods in order of nutritional value (e.g., least healthy comes first, followed by more healthy breakfast).
4. Discuss final sequences in relation to healthy eating habits, fruits, vegetables, minerals and vitamins necessary for healthy body functions.

A similar activity can be created with photographs of what the children did during the weekend (e.g., playing football, sitting by the computer and playing a video game, visiting grandparents). Discuss different body parts, heart rate and the importance of exercise to a healthy lifestyle.

Children who own their own tablet or smartphone can keep a digital diary of foods and activities at home (e.g., for a week) and share the results at school, swapping pictures and discussing what is more and what is less healthy for each individual child.

⊗ Be a researcher!

Our Story has been designed with young children in mind and the idea that children too can be researchers and learn through experimentation, testing hypotheses and self-discovery. Young researchers can tell their own stories and research reports in pictures, audio recordings or short videos. They can experience what it feels like to do their own research, by formulating a hypothesis, designing an experiment and carrying it out. The app contains a set of colourful templates illustrating the key steps in a research process (introduction, methods, analysis, discussion). You can either ask children to insert these templates within a given story sequence to help them see the sequence of a given research project or encourage them to conduct their own research project and use the headings to order the documentation of the experience. Discuss with children how it feels and what it takes to be a researcher and where scientific knowledge comes from. For structured sessions' plans to facilitate children's social science research, have a look at the Children's Research Centre website (at the Open University: www.open.ac.uk/researchprojects/childrens-research-centre/).

NOTE

1. In 2016, the Android version of Our Story was in the process of updating; we recommend using the free iPad version to benefit from full features of the app.

CHAPTER 7

Explain Everything
Really, explain anything and everything

Application

Explain Everything – an interactive screencasting whiteboard that enables the user to explain and demonstrate ideas, knowledge and learning through narration and description

Subject possibilities

Cross-curricular by sharing knowledge across, and within, subjects

Category

- Apple device (iPad/iPhone) – paid
- Android app – paid

WHAT THE APP DOES

Explain Everything is a simple, but incredibly powerful app to use. The interface is minimal with the tools placed down the left-hand side and at the bottom of the screen. The layout is similar to that of both Promethean and Smart whiteboards, which makes it an intuitive app for both teachers and children. The app allows the user to animate their thinking by presenting ideas visually, or by using audio recordings to voiceover presentations, video or text. The app's forward-facing camera means that presentations can be shared in real time with a recording function that allows the user to *'present'* their thinking to a live audience.

Getting to grips with the basics

At the bottom of the screen there are three separate toolbars: the navigation toolbar, the screen recording toolbar and a smaller share/save and home toolbar.

The navigation toolbar

Move from page to page and add further slides using the '+' button.

The screen recording toolbar

By pressing the red record button, the camera will become live; it will record every action drawn or object moved on the screen. There are advanced features such as the ability to see the timeline, overwrite and mix sections together.

Exporting content toolbar

This toolbar consists of three options. The first is the share option. You can export your Explain Everything project as:

- *a video file* – This will export the finished recording as a media file so it can then be inserted into a presentation or uploaded and embedded on the school website. By toggling the 'All slides' button, you can select the specific slides you wish to export.
- *a PDF file* – This file type can be read in most browsers and mobile devices as the PDF retains its formatting and organisation.
- *a static image* – the slide is exported as an image file and can be saved to the camera roll, emailed or saved to a cloud-based storage service such as Dropbox. By toggling the 'All slides' button, you can select the specific slides you wish to export.
- *a project* – This file is saved as an Explain Everything file, which can then be opened up by the app.

Some tools (pen, shapes, text) have additional actions behind them, which are accessed by holding your finger down on the icon and then the extra menu will appear.

THE APP IN CONTEXT

Being able to explain thinking and approaches to problems is hard to capture in print, as ideas are often complex. When you watch children explain the answer to a mathematical problem, they often point to numbers or shapes, moving back and forth in their thinking before revisiting and revising their initial ideas. Being able to share this level of thinking with the teacher is just one way of using Explain Everything – it allows children to listen, talk, show and demonstrate their working out. These skills can be transferred across subjects, and if children have their own school iPads, they can also create presentations at home as part of a homework topic; as such, it's an ideal app to bridge learning across home and school.

TEACHERS' USE IN CLASS

Explain Everything can be used by teachers, both as a pedagogical tool with a focus on creative and visual approaches to learning and teaching, and as a practical tool for presenting ideas and as an assessment mechanism. Rather than using a traditional PowerPoint to share ideas with children in a linear style, Explain Everything allows the presentation to move back and forth, and this is a useful approach when consolidating children's knowledge. Children can be encouraged to self-assess a piece of work by incorporating it into the app and narrating the specific aspects they would like to draw your attention to. The process is reciprocal; as you share your responses to the work, you are creating a shared and valuable dialogue.

ACTIVITIES

 **Maths problem-solving**

There are some excellent mathematical problems found in the 2000 National Strategies publication *Mathematical Challenges for Able Pupils in Key Stages 1 and 2* (http://webarchive.nationalarchives. gov.uk/20110202093118/http:/nationalstrategies.standards.dcsf.

gov.uk/node/85260) whereby the children can recreate the maths problem and then use Explain Everything to demonstrate their understanding. Present the problem to the children on the whiteboard, or using physical equipment. Ask the children to take a photograph of the practical problem and then use the app to record how to solve it.

Repeated addition

Challenge 29 explores the strategy of repeated addition, where the children have to make the total number of legs adding up to 23 using only Bipods (with two legs) and Tripods (with three legs).

- Ask the children to draw a Bipod and a Tripod on a scrap piece of paper.
- Press the '+' and then take a 'New photo' of the Bipod. Use the dotted lasso tool to cut out the image of the Bipod. Repeat the process for a Tripod.
- Once on the page, press the 'i' and then on a Bipod/Tripod. Select 'Duplicate' to reproduce the image. Whilst selected, you can press the duplicate option as many times as you wish and it will lay a duplicate image on top of the last one.
- To move the objects around, press the hand symbol. The children can then manipulate the images until they are able to solve the challenge.

Explain it to a friend

Children are often better at explaining how they have understood a concept or strategy if they use 'child-friendly' talk. Use the app to capture this explanation. For example, using the pen, ask a child to explain how to find 3/4 or 4/6 of an amount and how this can be achieved. The child's recording can then be used to support other children or uploaded to the class blog as 'Explanation of the week'.

Producing a screencast

A screencast is another name for a short video explaining how to do something and is accompanied by narration, which Explain Everything is perfect for.

Ask the children to use the app to create a two-minute video about a personal interest they have outside school. Two minutes is not very long, so the children will have to plan the points they are going to make, as well as sourcing images from home to use in their screencast. The planning process will require children to make notes, create a script and find a visual way to present their thinking. Ask the children to combine their images and narrate some of the things they enjoy about their activity; they may also include some useful facts e.g., how long they've been involved, if there is an element of training and whether any specialist equipment is required. Ask each child to record their screencast and upload their finished video that can then be watched by the rest of the class.

How to record and navigate the screen during a recording

1. Press the red record button to begin recording your narration. The first time you do this it will ask for access to your microphone which you will need to allow by pressing the 'OK' button.
2. The recorder will begin and the time counter will display how long the narration is. Encourage the children to create a skeleton script to aid their narration.
3. Whilst recording, the play button turns into a pause button in case the narration dries up or to collect thoughts. If you want to continue recording after the pause button has been pressed, then re-press the record button.

During the recording process, you can interact with the screen by:

a. *Moving and resizing images* around just by using your finger or pinching your thumb and finger together. This can be really useful when talking about multiple images. Resize the images to small thumbnail versions around the screen on one page and then when recording, move each image in turn to the middle, pinch and stretch out the image to fit the screen, talk about the image and then reduce the image down and place it back on the page.
b. *Use a pen* by selecting the pen tool and then drawing on the screen to either demonstrate understanding or to illustrate points in conjunction with the spoken narrative.

If your slideshow has multiple pages, then you can advance to each page whilst recording your narration by clicking the forward and back arrows located at either side of the slide number.

4. To stop the recording, press the red record button.
5. To play the recording, press the green play button (or a full-screen mode can be entered by pressing and holding the play button and then selecting the yellow play button).

Advanced features

• Click the time duration to reveal the recorded timeline. There are various editing features and the ability to lock parts of the timeline and split or delete parts of unwanted narration.
• Navigate the recorded material by sliding the timeline left and right.
• The last function allows you to overwrite or mix sections of the audio.

 Visual mental maths tests

Insert an image on to each slide. Using the record function, create a mental maths question for each slide and share the video in a place the children can easily access.

 Become the teacher

Children love to be the teacher and explain what they know. Use the app to describe any aspect of learning. Use the app to explain the key features of the water cycle (http://resources.woodlands-junior.kent.sch.uk/homework/swater.html). First, insert an image background or use the pen to draw a background for the water cycle. Pressing and holding down the pen will reveal the line thickness and different colours can be selected using the colour palette. To stop things moving around the screen, press on the 'i' and then press on the different elements and select 'Set as background'. With so many elements connected on the screen, it can be useful to lock to the back so that only a few elements (such as rain clouds) move about. Use the laser pointer and a different coloured pen that will stand out whilst narrating the process of the water cycle.

🔍 Such a doughnut! Bringing your instructions to life!

Combine photographs and videos to capture how to carry out a set of instructions, in this case for eating a doughnut. This is an unhealthy* option of course but great fun nevertheless! (* activity can be substituted for healthier options – further ideas for party games to play and write the instructions for can be found on www.activityvillage.co.uk/party-games).

During a unit of work on instructional writing, working in small groups of four, the pupils have to find different ways to eat a ring doughnut. Lay newspaper down to catch any 'spillages'. In the group, thread a piece of string through the doughnut as two children from the group stand either side and pull the string taut. As one child eats their doughnut off the line, another child photographs (and videos) the different stages using the camera app.

1. Load the Explain Everything app.
2. Select a new project so the whiteboard space is viewable.
3. Press the '+' button to insert a new object and then select the 'Photo, Video or File' option. Select the photo option that will then load the camera roll with your photos. Insert the first photograph. Just before it is placed on the page, you have a number of options to 'Edit the image'. Here you can crop, rotate and even use the lasso/freehand tool to trace around the image and cut it out. Pinch the image with your thumb and finger to resize and rotate the image. When complete, press 'Done' and the image is then inserted onto the page.
4. Press the new slide '+' in the bottom toolbar to add a new slide and then repeat the image adding stage until all the photographs and stages are complete.
5. Finally, record the narration for each image using procedural words and imperative verbs to enhance the writing. Provide the children with narration word bank sheets to support their spoken narrative.

Listen to me treasure hunt

Develop the children's listening skills by providing a physical piece of work or books for the children to look at when they are finding information on the sheet whilst clues are shared by you using the audio function.

Provide open-ended questions for the children to listen to and work through. For example:

[whilst recording, enlarge an image of Henry VIII] …

- *Look carefully at this photograph; it is an image of a Tudor king.*
- *Can you work out who he is using the books and information provided?*
- *Explore some more and find out if he was married and whether he had any children. Write down any information you collect.*
- *After you have finished writing down the information, return to this video for a further challenge.*

 Flipping the classroom

The flipped classroom (http://flippedinstitute.org/how-to-flip) is a pedagogic approach where children come to a lesson ready to talk about the learning they have already completed at home. For example, a short video clip is created about the next session with instructions for the children to prepare, think about and revise for the next day. Create a video in the app and select the 'Share' option (square with the vertical arrow), so the finished video can be uploaded (YouTube, Dropbox). Send a link or share with the pupils using an email with a link embedded in it or using Dropbox.

The flipped classroom concept is a good way of engaging the children with their learning before the session, which should, in theory, allow you to interact differently in the classroom: discussion; probing thinking and understanding of a topic; or, accelerating the lesson based on the children's prior knowledge. Prepare your videos in advance, pressing the red record button to record your narration.

The content does not always need to be created from scratch and there are many flexible ways of adding content into your video before you record. Press on the '+' option and navigate to the 'Photo, video or file' option. Connected cloud storage services (such as Dropbox, Google Drive, Box) work well given their ability to add PDF and PowerPoint files. Once the service is connected, navigate to the file and press on it to insert it into your Explain Everything project. The PowerPoint or PDF will load and each page will be placed on a separate page.

⊗ Creating digital stories

Create digital stories by inserting a background onto a slide. The image could be from a picture book, non-fiction book, or from the internet using a such as The Literacy Shed (www.literacyshed.com/the-images-shed.html) which has some useful starting points.

Although secondary focused, The English Tutor has some very good photographs which can be selected beforehand for the children to use (http://englishtutorhome2.blogspot.co.uk/2013/06/creative-writing-english-language-exam.html).

Save the images to the camera roll or to a shared Dropbox folder (for the children to access and select from later).

- Once the image has been located insert it onto a new slide.
- Next press the '+' button and select 'New photo'. Working with another person, ask the children to take a photograph of themselves to add to the scene. Once the photograph is taken, use the dotted-line lasso tool (the first option in the menu line) to cut out the person and then press 'Done.'
- This will insert the cut out at the top of the screen. Additional images taken by the camera or resources from the internet can then be brought into the software in the same way.
- Record the narration for the story, moving the characters across the screen.

⌖ Read and illustrate creative writing

Insert some text on to each slide using the text tool (the 'A' symbol). You may have to resize the box by pressing the blue adjustment arrows in the bottom right-hand corner so that the text spreads across the whole page. Ask the children to create a story or type in a creative piece of writing. Divide the sections of writing up evenly over the different slides. Return to the first slide and press 'Record'. Read the sentences using the pen to illustrate the story as you narrate. Pausing the recording and drawing in the detail will also accelerate the process.

⌒ Tell me a story, Mr Fox

Photograph a well-known story or historical character. Working with a partner, create an interview script and then record the interview from the point of view of that character with both people in role. For example, in the case of Roald Dahl's book *Fantastic Mr Fox* the interviewer could ask questions about which farmer was the easiest to steal from or which he enjoyed the most.

☀ A picture paints a thousand words

Insert a photograph that could be used to support mathematical investigation work. It could be an image whereby the children have to draw round as many 2D shapes as they see in the photograph or an image of a box of cereal and the children have to work out which is cheaper in an offer of buy-one-get-one free or two boxes for £2.60.

☀ Geography maps

Insert a photograph of a map. Use the Google Maps app (https://itunes.apple.com/gb/app/google-maps/id585027354?mt=8) to locate the local area. The map can be zoomed in or out by pinching the screen. Take a screenshot by holding down the on/off button and then pressing the home button on the iPad. The screenshot will be placed in the photo/camera roll. The children can use the annotate tool to trace their route to school whilst explaining some of the geographical features they observe on their way to school.

🥣 Creating a yearly happy digital scrapbook

After each topic, create a digital scrapbook by using the camera and video options within the app. During the conclusion of the topic, the children can record a video and include any piece of work created. This could be work on display, or found in different exercise books, or physical objects they have made. Record a video to evaluate the parts of the projects they enjoyed and are proud of.

These videos can be resized so they do not take up the space of the entire slide. Take photographs and add them to the scrapbook.

Extension activity

Ask the children to export their finished video of their favourite topic moments to a shared place. Then organise each clip into individual folders. As the year progresses, repeat the digital scrapbook activity until you have as many clips as you wish. At the end of the year (and with some assistance), collect these individual reflections and then burn them on to a DVD, one set of reflections for each individual. These 'Happy Digital Scrapbook DVDs' could then be sent home as a present for families at the end of the year.

Did you hear me?

Ask each child to take an image of the book they are reading. Challenge the children to record themselves reading either independently or with the assistance of another adult. Play the recording back and listen and assess the child's fluency and expression so you can guide their next steps.

Show me what you know assessments

Use the app to collect evidence about pupil progress or understanding of a topic. In a maths assessment on number bonds to ten, use the shape tool to place ten shapes onto the top or bottom of the slide page. Use the text tool to write the name of the child onto the page. Press the record button, and ask the child to explain how different pairs of numbers equal ten. The child can then drag the objects around the page whilst counting aloud.

This strategy can be varied depending on the content matter. For historical work, insert the dates and images of historic events on the slide. The children have to place these in chronological order whilst explaining their reasons for their choices.

Guiding the drafting and redrafting process

Use the photocopier or scanner or take a photograph of a child's work. During your recording, use the annotation options to show

how the work has been marked, or create an exemplar with an accompanying analysis of the effective/interesting aspects of the work. This should help children to understand what a marker is looking for and how to improve their work.

I missed that input ...

If you are feeling professionally brave, use the app as a record of your teaching. Import your PowerPoint or use the app as a mini-whiteboard. During the teaching process, press the record button and record the entire input. When you have finished teaching, if a child missed the input or was absent, they can watch the lesson again just by playing the Explain Everything file.

Sharing children's work

Explain Everything works well for demonstrating and for verbal work. Therefore, there are a number of uses where children can demonstrate their knowledge or use it for creative writing. Use the app to take a photograph of a piece of children's work. This could be a very good example or with the child's permission an example whery you assist them in improving their work.

- Press on the '+' button and then 'New photo'.
- Take a photograph of the piece of work.
- Then press the 'i' button and either navigate to the Lock menu and select the top option (Lock) or navigate to the Edit option and press 'Set as background'.
- Now record your narration by pressing 'Record'. By locking the piece of work in place, this will mean that you can annotate the work freely without the work moving.
- Once finished, export the work by pressing the 'Share' button then exporting the video to the camera roll/photos.
- During the lesson input, plug in an adapter to the mobile device (VGA or HDMI connector) to display the video to the children. Alternatively, if you have connected an AppleTV to your projector then the image can be sent to the screen using AirPlay.

OBSERVATIONS OF PUPIL PROGRESS

With the ability to attach images, videos and text and annotate on the screen, use the app during 'Learning Walks' around the school when observing classroom learning. The app is a quick and easy way to record examples of good work, good practice or videos of children's progress. Use one slide for each observation and collect on the screen observations that might be missed.

CELEBRATING A CHILD'S ACHIEVEMENT

Take a photograph of a child's piece of work using the camera. Use the text tool to write the words 'CONGRATULATIONS, YOU'VE BEEN A HARD WORKING STAR THIS WEEK!!!' Make an animated card by asking another adult, for example, a teaching assistant, to film a short video with the child and yourself where you point out their hard work and achievements. Ask the child how they feel about their work. Insert the video into the slide, then record the whole screen. Expand the recording by asking a person to record a 'well done' audio message. Export and send the completed video to the child's parent, so they can celebrate their achievement.

CHAPTER 8

Do Ink Green Screen

Imagine away your classroom

Application

Do Ink Green Screen

Subject possibilities

Drama

Category

- Apple device (iPad/iPhone) – paid

WHAT THE APP DOES

Do Ink produce two apps which work well together or as separate apps in their own right. Do Ink's Green Screen app allows up to three images and videos to be stitched together. Green screening allows you to take a video or image against a flat coloured background (green and blue work particularly well, hence the name) and then lay that on top of another image. The magic happens when a **chroma key** filter is applied. The chroma key filters out the colour to reveal the image or video below. As well as the ability to insert an image or video there is also the option to import an animation made in Do Ink's animation app (see Chapter 12). All the equipment needed apart from the app is a green screen (for example, Kudlian software, or see YouTube clips to create your own for DIY version). Ensure that the screen is flat and has an even distribution of light. You may have to add additional lighting to achieve the desired effect as if there are patches of shadows it will make the background look uneven when the chroma key is applied.

THE APP IN CONTEXT

Using a green screen is an ideal way for children to interact with activities that require them to use spoken language in a way that engages with their audience, as well as offering them the chance to both perform and evaluate their own dramatic presentations. Making backgrounds come to life, children can go beyond imagining themselves in a favourite film or book by actually entering that imagined world. The ideas don't need to be too complicated or technical, for example, familiar hotseating strategies can come to life in a green screen setting. Year 3 children can take on the role of characters from favourite books, like Charlie and his adventures in the chocolate factory or Wilbur in *Charlotte's Web*. Children can be encouraged to ask questions of their favourite characters, or take on the role of a TV presenter by reporting on key events from literature or historical events.

TEACHERS' USE IN CLASS

Key for teachers when planning creative work, particularly for writing, is to find a hook that will inspire and enthuse. The use of a green screen will grab the attention of any child at the start of a topic, especially if their teacher suddenly appears on the big screen in the role of an explorer or forensic scientist. Even teachers who are slightly wary of big drama activities can find a way of using the green screen, especially if it can be prepared in advance with the help of willing colleagues. Green screen activities can also be used as a way of introducing visitors or new pupils to the school by taking them on a virtual tour of the buildings.

ACTIVITIES

💭 Hotseating – interviewing a character from a book

Using the camera app, take a photo of the front cover of a favourite book, fiction or non-fiction. Use the green screen background and film a book review by talking to the audience in a *Jackonory*-style (see YouTube) or straight-to-camera piece. Another idea would be to film an interview between two children with one of the children taking on the role of the main character.

🔍 Goldilocks and the three bears: guilty or not guilty? The trial continues ...

Draw or find images of a courtroom, a bowl of porridge, a selection of chairs of various heights and a selection of beds. Using the green screen and working in a group, film the prosecution and defence case for whether Goldilocks should go to jail. When it comes to the witness statements, make or use finger puppets of Goldilocks and the three bears.

🔍 What's the weather like?

Create a film of an animated weather report. Think carefully about where you direct the children to stand in the role of weather reporter, as this will affect how the map is animated. Leave enough space around so as not to obscure the map image; it's worth taking a quick photograph using the tablet's camera to see how much of the screen is left. Use masking tape to place an 'x' or a box on the floor so the reporter knows how much they can move around.

Create a script for the weather report, typing directly into the notes app so you know how the weather report will progress. Create the animation by placing a map with weather symbols into the Explain Everything app (see Chapter 7). You can create your own maps or use resources from the internet to help with the symbols and maps. Primary Resources (www.primaryresources.co.uk/geography/ geography1.htm) has a section on weather and tourism that may help.

Once the animated film is complete, export it to the camera roll. To record the weather presenter's narration, record the film against the green screen using the camera app. To make this easier for the presenter, you could place a projector behind the camera with the weather script or write the main points on a piece of paper which can act as autocue, so that it will be easier to remember.

Once both parts are created/filmed, load the app and begin a new project by clicking the '+' button and selecting 'Create a new project'. When the project loads, there are three lines within the timeline; build from the bottom line first.

Place your animated map on the bottom line by pressing the '+' to the right of the line. Select the source (camera, video, image or a Do Ink animation). In this instance it is a piece of video from the camera roll. Press the video source and the camera roll will load. In the topic left-hand corner there is also a 'Locations' option so you can also import video stored in cloud storage apps such as Dropbox.

Once the film is pressed it will load into the bottom timeline. Next, repeat the same process but on the second timeline insert the video with the chroma screen background. When the chroma screen video is added over the top, then use the chroma background tools to fine-tune the green screen out, in order to reveal the weather map animation below.

Working with the chroma background

To the right of the timeline there are three tools for adjusting the images you are working with:

- *Chroma tool* – this option produces a 'chroma colour wheel' with the video image above. To the left, the screen shows the finished result. On the video image above the colour wheel, press on the green screen in the picture and the majority of the background will disappear. By sliding the sensitivity slide on the right-hand side the main objects will become clearer on the screen.

- *Crop tool* – if you have an occasion where you haven't quite filmed the whole screen and can see the edges of the green screen frame or the rest of the classroom at the sides then selecting the crop tool will allow you to grab the yellow corners and crop the image.
- *Mask tool* – this tool provides a set of tools so you can create a mask and rub out parts of the green screen or the image. This is extremely useful if you are using a puppet and wish to remove the arm in the shot so you are just left with the puppet moving.
  - The **magic wand** will paint out any colour matching it in the image. So if you press on the brown desk and adjust the sensitivity anything of the same colour will disappear, revealing the bottom image.
  - The **eraser tool** lets you rub out sections that are not required such as the hand of a puppeteer. If you make a mistake, then the **paint brush** will repaint what was there.
  - The **rectangle and ellipse tool** will draw those shapes on to the screen. Anything in the video that passes over these shapes will not be shown.

 Dr Science reports on an investigation

Using the camera app, film the stimulus for the beginning of an experiment. It could be a 'Have you ever noticed … ?' type video to encourage the children's possibility thinking. For example, have you ever noticed when you are out shopping and use one of the supermarket's bags to carry your shopping, some bags are better at carrying large amounts of weight, whilst others break the very second you leave the exit?

Use the green screen technique (outlined above) to film yourself in the role of Dr Science. Explain to the children the task (in character) and how you would like them to complete the investigation.

 Telling stories from different cultures

Film the children against a green screen background retelling either a well-known story from another culture or a story they have adapted using a story structure. Useful starting points can be found in Pie Corbett's *Bumper Books of Story Telling into Writing* for Key Stage 1 and Key Stage 2 (see references).

Historical reporting

Select from your history topic a key event and produce a news broadcast reporting on the event: for example, the day the tomb of Tutankhamen was discovered by Howard Carter; the death of Henry VIII with a review of his life; or the life and times of ordinary people during World War II. You may already have access to images and clips through specific software subscriptions at school but also explore the resources from British Pathe (www.britishpathe. com/pages/education). This is a film and newsreel archive with video from 1896 to 1976; it contains over 85,000 individual films as well as 12 million still images.

Recounting experiences – a tour around the school

Take videos of places around the school a new pupil may visit during their first few weeks at their new school. Use the green screen to narrate a commentary introducing the pupils to the school. This could be used as a transition project or as a way of promoting the school. Pupils could interview senior members of staff in their office/classroom and use iMovie to edit the clips together. They will need to export the green screen clips to the camera roll in order to use them in iMovie (see below).

Exporting your green screen video

From the main screen, press the 'Save' option next to the play button. This will immediately begin the exporting process. When completed, you will be asked whether you would like to 'Preview your video', 'Show the export options' i.e. send it in an email, AirDrop, notes or iCloud sharing and finally the ability to 'Save to the camera roll'. Press on the 'Save to the camera roll' option and your finished green screen video will be available to use.

Create a modern foreign language video

Against the green screen, record a narration introducing the children to the pronunciation of different colours or conversation phrases in French/Spanish/German. Behind the green screen layer on the Do Ink timeline, click the '+' button and place images from the camera roll that illustrate the words spoken by the person in front of the green screen.

It's a bug's life ... life down under

Now is your chance to become the David Attenborough of your school. Using the mobile device, venture out into the school grounds and film different habitats and creatures found around the school grounds. Collect a variety of photographs and film footage. Against the green screen, film a scientific commentary explaining what was found, where, what it is and how it can be identified.

REFERENCES

Corbett, P. (2006). *Bumper Book of Story Telling into Writing at Key Stage 1*. Melksham: Clown Publishing.

Corbett, P. (2007). *Bumper Book of Story Telling into Writing at Key Stage 2*. Melksham: Clown Publishing.

LINKED WEBSITES

https://itunes.apple.com/gb/app/green-screen-by-do-ink/id730091131?mt=8&ign-mpt=uo%3D4

https://itunes.apple.com/gb/app/animation-drawing-by-do-ink/id364762290?mt=8&ign-mpt=uo%3D4

www.kudlian.net/products/screen/index.php

CHAPTER 9

Padlet

Collaboration starting with a blank page

Application

Padlet

Subject possibilities

Primary foreign languages

Category

- Apple device (iPad/iPhone) – free
- Android app – free

Paid options are available for additional security and privacy options.

WHAT THE APP DOES

Padlet is a collaborative app, and it works in much the same way as Google documents, in that users are able to contribute to the same project. However, a key difference is that Padlet works like an online wall of information providing a range of backgrounds and photo upload options and it combines text postings, visual images, video and comment options. Users can create multiple walls across a range of subject options, and whilst content can be added by anyone from any device, it is the wall owner who has the editing rights, which means that any potential collaborators can only edit/delete their own contributions. The school *Backpack* option enables the teacher to set privacy options so that only approved users can add/see the virtual wall of shared information.

THE APP IN CONTEXT

Padlet is a flexible app, which enables the user to personalise their walls through creative modifications and additions; for example, in English, children could add a text-based background as the wallpaper for their Padlet on word choices, or synonyms for over-used words like 'big' or 'said'. The collaborative nature of the app also means that as a teacher you can set children the challenge to add to a wall you create. In mathematics, KS1 children could seek out examples of familiar shapes, take photographs of what they find and then post these to a 'Shape Padlet'. As well as the visual image, children could also add a short text or caption.

In KS2, Padlet could be used to reinforce vocabulary learning in language studies; in French, children could be introduced to new vocabulary and set the challenge to create sticky notes to use the word in context. As the notes are limited to 150 characters, the children need to be concise and precise in their sentence construction. Teachers can then assess language learning and provide feedback or extension activities within the same Padlet. What about asking children to research the languages spoken in school and to create greetings in the multiple languages which can then be shared on the school website as a 'Welcome' page to new visitors?

TEACHERS' USE IN CLASS

Padlet provides the space for teachers and pupils to contribute to ongoing learning walls. The teacher can create a Padlet for each pupil which can then be accessed throughout the year, and where pupils can add their own sticky notes on reflections on their learning, or post a photograph or key piece of learning, which can then form the basis of a pupil conference. Because the Padlet goes across a range of subjects and throughout the year, it will give an accurate visual of the learning and provide a creative starting point for discussions about learning and progress. Padlet could also be a useful hub of teacher development, through the creation of post-CPD/staff meeting feedback. Staff could add their immediate reflections or next steps in response to staff input on new initiatives or agreed school objectives.

ACTIVITIES

 Digital etiquette

As part of a digital citizenship programme, and before collaborating, establish some ground rules with your class concerning what a good post should look like – which types of photograph are acceptable (no selfies) as well as acknowledging where images or text sources come from.

 Moderating posts

By pressing the 'Share with collaborators' icon, you are able to set the Padlet link's privacy and copy the link to the clip as well as invite collaborators by inputting their email address. The final option is to 'Moderate posts'. If this option is toggled on, then all posts will require an administrator or editor of the Padlet to approve the post before it appears publicly. When this option is on, the child will see a yellow message informing them that their post is awaiting approval whilst the original creator of the Padlet (or an editor) is presented with an option to either approve the post or remove it. This works particularly well and adds an additional layer of safeguarding if you have embedded the Padlet on a website and are asking for views from say the whole school community.

 What do we think about this subject?

Explore the use of Padlet by collecting views on a subject at the beginning of a topic. Padlet is a useful tool for adding layers to an activity. Padlet provides a working space for the children to move their thoughts around and play with the information through their fingertips on the page. For example, you can find out what the children know about a new history topic. Ask the children to note down the thoughts and ideas they already have about the Romans. Ask the children to click the '+' button at the bottom of the screen to add a new post to their own individual board (you can also double tap anywhere on the screen). Ask the children to write a title and then add their thoughts underneath where it says 'Write something …'.

Underneath the description are a number of icons to be able to attach content to the Padlet note. (See 'What media can I add?') Using books from the library, ask the children to photograph images to support their thoughts. Finally, using the books, tell the children to add new facts to their own individual Padlets.

⊗ Let's find out together

As well as being used as an individual tool, Padlet also provides the opportunity to work collaboratively and add to shared projects in the same way you would collaborate using GoogleDocs (www. google.co.uk/docs/about) and PrimaryPad (http://primarypad. com).

- Set up a new Padlet.
- Press the 'Share' button in the bottom right-hand corner of the screen (the square with the vertical arrow). There are numerous options for being able to share a Padlet:

  - By email – Send the link to the child's email address or the shared email address the mobile device uses.
  - Embedding the html code – Embed the code into blogs, websites or interactive whiteboard software programs.
  - QR code – One of the quickest ways for children to add their comments to a Padlet is to connect your teacher mobile to your interactive whiteboard so the app can be seen and then press 'View QR code' (Chapter 4). The children will need the app installed on their own device but do not necessarily need an account. At the bottom of the loading screen is the option to 'Continue as guest'. By pressing this, the children are presented with two options. The children can either type the Padlet web address in or press 'Scan QR code'. By pressing this option, they then hold their device up to the board where the code is and the Padlet will load (providing there is wifi access).

Provide a topic for the children to research and add their ideas to.

👤 You be the judge

Present a dilemma to the children, which they will have to present information about – should Goldilocks be sent to prison for the hideous crimes she committed?

Double tap to add a new note and write in the title box *'Should go to prison'* and in a separate box write *'Should not go to prison'*. Move the headings to opposite sides of the page. Ask the children to present their arguments by providing appropriate evidence and placing it on the correct side.

👤 Let's have a heated debate!

Use Padlet to structure a debating lesson. Provide the children with a topic to debate, for example:

- Should a new shopping centre replace part of the playground?
- Should animals be kept in a cage?
- Is texting whilst driving wrong?
- Should technology be moderated for children in the same way bedtimes are?
- Should texting be allowed at the dinner table?
- Should everybody in the school be able to not wear school uniform one day a week?

Divide the class into different roles – arguments for and against the topic. Place two labels 'for' and 'against' on the page. Ask the children to collaborate in their groups to present their initial thoughts. Ask the children to create one post on the Padlet page that states their position clearly. Discuss both these posts as a class.

Ask the children to use a child-friendly search engine:

- Safe Search Kids: www.safesearchkids.com
- SafeSearch: http://primaryschoolict.com
- KidRex: www.kidrex.org
- Google Junior: www.googlejunior.com

The children will need to search and find supporting information for their arguments, for and against. When they have finished, review the information presented. Have any of the points been strengthened? Are there any new points that have been added?

Ask the children to explain their thoughts. What do they think? Has anyone changed his or her mind? Can the children defend their answers? In light of the debate do the children need to refine their original statement?

What do the main characters have in common?

Select four well-known texts the majority of the children will have read. Insert a photograph of each of the books in the middle of the page. Ask the children to post a new note describing any similarities they notice about the main characters or the good characters versus the bad characters.

What media can I add?

When the 'add an attachment' button is pressed, you have two options: add a link from a piece of media found on the web, or upload from a cloud-based storage service or the camera.

You can link to any media found on a website if you have the URL website address. This includes websites, pages from a website, YouTube videos, documents, newspaper articles, other Padlets ... in fact, anything on the web. Copy the website address (www.bbc.co.uk) and then press 'Submit'. A preview will be generated so a pictorial thumbnail is shown. Pressing on the image will then load in the screen. If the media fails to load, then pressing on 'View original' will load the attachment in the mobile internet browser.

'Upload/use camera' will present the camera and photo library (camera roll) option where you can take a photograph/video or insert one you have taken before. If you have the Dropbox app installed and 'logged in' then this option will also appear in the menu list. This means that any file you are able to load to Dropbox can be inserted into the Padlet. Therefore, the range of information and media children can access is staggering.

Reviewing the situation

Use Padlet to review the children's learning and knowledge at the end of a topic; this may include the highlights and elements of the unit they have enjoyed the most or those aspects they did not enjoy. If you wish the comments to be private, then whilst creating the Padlet toggle the action to 'Moderate posts' (found when the 'Share with collaborators' icon is pressed).

At the end of the activity, press the 'Share/export' icon and then press 'Open in Safari' which will then load the Padlet in a web browser. The Padlet settings bar is located on the right-hand side. Click the fourth icon down, the 'Share' option, and from here you access the various options of sharing the data in the same way as you can through the app. However, there is one difference – there is an option to export the Padlet data to an Excel spreadsheet, which is useful when collecting whole school responses on a subject area, as the familiar Excel functions can filter or graph statistical information.

⊗ Wonder working walls

Set up a Padlet and encourage the children to post questions about the topic they are studying so they can search for the answers. The activity provides a useful starting point for circle time or P4C (Philosophy for Children) activities. Print the QR code of the Padlet and place it in a prominent place in your classroom. To do this, press the 'Share/export' icon and then scroll the bottom options until the 'View QR code' option is visible. Once pressed in the top right-hand corner there is a second share/export option that then allows you to email the QR code or print it via AirPrint.

⌒ Find me an example of ...

During a science topic focusing on solids, liquids and gases, place three new notes entitled 'Solids' – with a picture of some ice cubes; 'Liquids' – with a picture of some water; and 'Gases' – showing the steam portion of the kettle boiling. The children then walk around the school finding real-life examples of solids, liquids and gases and posting them around the relevant label.

👤 Best work examples

Throughout a topic, ask the children to post an example of a piece of work they are particularly proud of. Provide a link or embed the Padlet onto the class blog so parents can see how the topic and indeed the children's work are progressing.

🥣 Book reviews

Ask the children to take a photograph at the beginning of the book they are reading. At the end of each chapter, ask the children to add to the Padlet a summary of the main action and their thoughts on the book. This could also be an activity parents could complete as part of a homework task if the link is shared with them. At the end of the book, if evidence is required, the children can press the 'Share/export' icon and then scroll through the options to the end until the 'Export as PDF' option appears. Once selected, a second 'Share/export' appears where the PDF can be emailed or printed via AirPrint.

☁ New year learning resolutions

At the beginning of January or September, ask the children to add their new year's learning resolution to the Padlet. What will you do differently this year?

👤 Kind words, kind thoughts

After a special trip or visitor to the school, ask the children to collect the thoughts they would like to share and then send the Padlet link along with the thank you card. Alternatively, after all the kind words have been expressed on the posts, go to the bottom right-hand icons and press the 'Share' icon. Scroll through the options until you reach 'Export as image' or 'Export as PDF'. Depending on how the answers have been posted, you may need to press the 'Settings' icon (the cog in the bottom right-hand side of the screen) and then scroll down to the layout options. Select either 'Stream' or 'Grid' which will organise the information in a different way.

OTHER APPS

Coacheye

CHAPTER 10

Scratch

Coding, computational thinking and problem-solving

Application

Scratch is a visual programming language, recently released as an app for mobile devices.

Subject possibilities

Mathematics, Science, Computing

Category

- Android app – free Scratch Junior for 5–7-year-olds
- Apple device (iPad/iPhone/iPod Touch) – free Scratch Junior

---

WHAT THE APP DOES

According to the Scratch creators from the Massachusetts Institute of Technology, Scratch is not only a creative but also an empowering tool because it broadens the range of what children can do on a computer: children can 'design and create on the computer, making it easier to combine graphics, photos, music, and sound into interactive creations' (http://scratched.gse.harvard.edu/sites/default/files/creating-with-scratch.pdf). The user interface of Scratch Junior is very similar to the visual programming website: there is a main activity area in the middle which features the result of an animation (e.g., a moving object, simulation, story or game). In the bottom, a filmstrip (similar to that of the Our Story app, see Chapter 6) contains small thumbnails with arrows indicating movements, and the possibility to add sounds or customised objects/animals. You can also add your own backgrounds and objects (tap the paintbrush or picture icon). Each new project is called a 'sprite'. If children don't access Scratch from the Scratch Junior app, they will need to create an account on the Scratch website to have their personal creating space.

ALTERNATIVE APPS

In addition to Scratch, other programming languages are available for young students. *Snap* (http://snap.berkeley.edu/) isn't available as a tablet/iPad app, but can be accessed through the website browser from any device. It is an easy-to-use and visually appealing coding platform where students can 'build their own blocks' of code, put these into scripts and see the program play them as a finished piece of animation.

For younger children, *Hopscotch* and *Daisy the Dinosaur* are free apps available for tablets and iPads, emulating the Scratch user interface. Children can drag and drop blocks into scripts, which generate an animation (by pressing the 'Play' button). There is also the possibility to add custom objects and events to enrich the user-generated codes. *Daisy the Dinosaur* is better suited for the lower end of KS2, featuring a dinosaur which moves across the screen according to the code.

THE APP IN CONTEXT

Anyone familiar with the UK Code Clubs would know about Scratch. If not, you have probably heard of the programming language as part of the coding curriculum. From September 2014, Information and Communications Technology (ICT) has been replaced by the so-called computing curriculum in the UK, which requires that children create and debug programs, understand concepts such as variables and sequencing and use logical reasoning skills when browsing the internet. Search skills and knowing how to use the internet to locate and evaluate information are assessed as part of the curriculum too.

Scratch can be used to teach some of these skills, including basic programming skills (which can be used later when programming with Python or Java), collaboration and creativity (especially when using the online community element accompanying the Scratch website). The Scratch website makes it possible for projects to be shared across the globe and for the community members to comment on and add to existing animations and games. This website is currently not available for mobile devices, so if children create their projects on tablets, make sure they share their finished versions via email so that they can be added to the community bank of projects via a desktop computer.

ACTIVITIES

The creators of Scratch provide a comprehensive guide to ideas and programming options with the programming language, freely available from this site: http://scratched.gse.harvard.edu/guide/. A periodically updated, user-generated guide is available from the Scratch community of users, who upload and share their creations online free of charge. You can share stories, exchange resources and learn more about Scratch uses by joining the community here: http://scratched.gse.harvard.edu/. Individual simple codes (e.g., making an object speak, change colour, move, dance, animate, etc.) are provided in a set of free cards which can be downloaded (and printed and cut out) or simply viewed on the Scratch Cards website: https://scratch.mit.edu/help/cards/. The cards are useful prompts to guide children through their explorations.

 Visualise processes

Use Scratch to visualise complex procedures and concepts, for example the water cycle or food chain as part of the KS2 Science curriculum. Ask the children to explore the key concept of sequence in Maths by telling the program what to do and translating a number sequence into a simple computer code.

1. 'Snap' together several blocks of graphics, photos or even sounds by tapping on the individual icons you wish to put into a sequence.
2. Ask the children to create a command, by dragging a block from the blocks area on the right side of the screen to the creating area.
3. Finished projects can be shared in the online community on the Scratch website, or on a personal webpage (just copy and embed the URL of a project).

Don't worry if the children take longer with the different Scratch blocks. The goal of the activity is experimentation, so dragging and dropping various blocks into the scripting area and then pulling them away is the whole point of the activity, enabling children to see how individual elements produce an action. It's the language around the activity and the mathematical vocabulary they use when exploring these relationships that really count.

Animate your own story!

1. Let the children design their own characters who can move, wear clothes and speak. Children can start by using the character templates available in the Scratch Library, or they can download characters created by other community users or created by them.
2. Ask the children to create characters who represent a particular historic event or a story you shared in the English class.
3. Ask the children to share their characters between each other and include one character in each other's stories.
4. Remixing their stories, ask children to compare their new stories to the original story. What has changed and what has made the story stronger/weaker? How does the animation add to the written text in a book?

Five random facts about ...

Combine any subject with the computing curriculum by encouraging children to find five miscellaneous facts about an English writer, historic period or endangered animal and include these in an animated presentation.

1. Create five backdrops, with each providing a template for one of the five random facts.
2. Encourage children to add a title page by using the Paintbrush button and fill in the templates (they can add the facts in text or as audio files).
3. The project can be remixed by other students adding five random facts about their chosen character/animal/historic period, adding to the length of the sprite.
4. If you prefer to remix an existing project, you can use the template provided by the Scratch Community, see: https://scratch.mit.edu/projects/10014866/#player.

Debug it!

Bugs happen and are a natural by-product of coding and programming. Therefore, mastering the coding skills is as much about knowing how to fix a program as it is about knowing how to code. This is why the creators of Scratch included several units with programs where the children can practise their debugging skills. Children need to spot the mistake (e.g., why is a cat not dancing when the space bar is tapped?), write down their solution and remix the program with it, so that it works as it should. Try a debugging exercise with the children by letting them choose one of the challenges in the *Debug it Scratch Studio*: http://scratch.mit.edu/studios/475483.

OTHER APPS

Flip Flap Safari

This app is not a coding app, but can be used in the context of computational thinking and relating coding to literacy activities. Flip Flap Safari was developed by Nosy Crow and has won the UKLA inaugural Children's Digital Book Award for 6–8-year-olds, judged in the UK entirely by teachers. Although the topic and content of the app may appear to be for younger children, the actual use of the app can be adjusted to the KS2 curriculum.

By creating various versions of animals, the children can apply their phonic knowledge and match made-up names of animals to correct spelling. Animal names will also extend children's understanding of words and how to use them in their writing. Creative thinking can be supported by encouraging children to make up their own new animals or use those suggested by their friends. The rhyme element will guide their choices, which can be nicely incorporated into a poetry lesson.

Dino Tales

Dino Tales is another app chosen by teachers in the context of the UKLA Children's Digital Book Award. Dino Tales can be used in English classes where children can edit text in the Dino stories. In the process of reading the tales, the app records the child's engagement and personalises the story ending for them. Such a feature can be discussed with children in the context of algorithms and coding. Personalised stories can be used to encourage children's independent reading but also to assess their understanding of the story. Children of all ages love to have their own dinosaur and take it on a journey where they can change the story context and the dinosaur's main characteristics (e.g., dinosaurs' colour, pattern and name).

CHAPTER 11

Puppet Pals
I Can Animate

Applications

Puppet Pals, Toontastic and I Can Animate

Subject possibilities

Art

Category

- Apple device (iPad/iPhone) – paid
- Android app – Toontastic – free

WHAT THE APP DOES

Children have long been fascinated by animation and the idea that imagined characters can somehow come to life. Before today's technology, children used flick books to create moving cartoon strips, or the rather laborious process of taking single camera images that could be turned into movie strips with Plasticine® characters appearing to have a life of their own. Some of you will remember the original Morph, created by Tony Hart for the *Take Hart* and *Hartbeat* television shows; whilst the Morph of the 21st century is rather slicker than the original, you can still upload and view user-generated Morph stories on the Aardman site, home of Wallace and Gromit. The I Can Animate app uses stop-frame animation to enable the user to create their own movies, and it is an easy and accessible way for children to imagine the storytelling process in a visual and animated way.

THE APP IN CONTEXT

The application is easy to use across both key stages and all subjects, but is particularly useful for Art. The key skills of imagination and creativity are at the heart of any story making or telling process and this type of app scaffolds the sequencing process and develops children's imagined thinking. For example, if recreating a well-known story or adding an unexpected twist in the plot, children will need to imagine what comes before and what comes after and how best to represent that. They may use Lego® characters or make their own soft clay models, but they will need to imagine what might happen next and to engage with possibility thinking. In Year 6, the app can support children in art lessons by allowing them to experiment with how different materials behave and how they can be manipulated with light to create different effects.

TEACHERS' USE IN CLASS

There are a number of ways that animation might be used for you as the teacher. You could animate your classroom rules; add a photograph of yourself to the background of your classroom; and narrate and demonstrate the expectations in your class: for example, how to tidy up the book corner, how to use scissors or you could use animation as a hook or stimulus for any number of lessons. A transition animation project could also be set up across infant/junior or junior/secondary school by taking children on a guided tour of the school and classrooms. Before joining your class in September, children could upload photographs of themselves and this could be turned into 'the class of 2016', encouraging a sense of belonging in a fun and creative way.

ACTIVITIES

⊗ Animating in different mediums and different light sources

Try experimenting with different types of materials to animate with. Fill a box with sand and use straws, fingers or brushes to make marks on the screen. Take images at every step of the way to avoid shots of arms coming into the frame. As an alternative to using sand, try using paper, paint and straws to create firework animations. You will need a makeshift stand to secure the iPad in place. Use lamps and lights to illuminate the sand or paper otherwise the iPad shadow can make the animation quite dark.

As a different technique, you can create a lightbox from a frame: place a piece of Perspex® on top and place lights underneath. The light shining through will create the animation effect.

◯ Tell me a story

Use the I Can Animate or Animate It apps to animate an imagined story. Use characters made out of modelling clay to retell a well-known traditional story or a fairy tale. You can animate a story with any number of objects you have around the classroom (modelling clay, shapes, handmade drawings). Before beginning to animate your story, consider the following:

- How will you set out your animation scene?
- Will you have a simple background? Complicated? Handmade, as part of an art project?
- What will you make the characters out of? Lego®? Clay? Foam pieces?
- What is the theme of your animation?
- How will you go about animating your work? There are some great tips to explore on the Animate It website (http://animate-it.com/category/get-animating/animation-tips/).

> To begin animating, set up your scene and before loading the app, place the tablet on a stand, so the camera can capture the figures. Try to ensure the camera stays still as you move the characters on the screen. Once set, press the large red button on the right-hand side of the screen. This will capture an image/frame.

As soon as you move the characters, a ghost image will appear. This is called **onion-skinning**, which allows you to animate in a much smoother way, as you can see the last image you captured. Keep taking photographs until you have completed your animation. Play the animation by pressing the 'Play' button in the bottom left-hand corner. To delete a frame, press on the frame at the bottom of the screen and press 'Delete'. You can also duplicate frames with the same action.

💬 Image springboard

Explore the use of an image to stimulate the children's interest and story writing. Use sites such as 'Animation Backgrounds' or the 'Take One Picture initiative' as starting points. There is a wealth of teacher-generated content on the TES Staffroom site, as well as on the Pinterest app; search the collections or type in key words such as 'big writing'.

Ask children to think about the setting shown in the image and ask them to imagine what may be happening in the image. What type of story would they animate from this image? Ask the children to mindmap on paper or use an app, such as Popplet, and then use their ideas to create a storyboard.

💡 On the big screen

Play the children an animated film to inspire their animation. For example, *Laughing Moon* (Kiyoshi Nishimoto, Japan 2000) from the British Film Institute's 'Starting Stories' resource (https://he.palgrave.com/page/detail/?sf1=barcode&st1=9781844572618) explores the use of shapes to tell a story. Use small 2D shapes in school or foam shapes purchased from the children's section of a supermarket to animate with.

🥣 Traditional stories with a twist

Take a traditional fairytale story or seek inspiration for a less well-known folktale from Pie Corbett's *Bumper Book of Story Telling into Writing* (2006, 2007). Draw a story map on paper or use drawing apps such as Tayasui Sketches Paper or Procreate Map to storyboard the main parts of the story and ask the children to embellish the story to make it different from the original by using different colours. For example, they might change the characters or setting or add or delete key points from the plotline. Use the story map to produce an animation of a tale with a twist.

Number bonds

Using ten objects and two different pieces of coloured paper, film the different ways of making number bonds to ten. The two different pieces of coloured paper can show the different pairs of numbers. During the animation, the children use number cards to form each possible calculation, using a small piece of modelling clay to create the addition sign.

 Time lapse

Have you ever noticed in an advert or television programme how a piece of film depicting a plant growing, or the seemingly magical construction of a skyscraper, appears to happen over the course of a couple of minutes, rather than over days or months?

The answer is the use of the time lapse setting. A sequence of photographs is taken over the course of a set duration (morning, day, week, month) and then exported to an app such as iMovie, before adding a suitable soundtrack. A good example is BBC's 'Snails Time-lapse – The Great British Year: Episode 3 Preview' (www.youtube. com/watch?v=acuoZeILLiE). Those who are squeamish should look away but children will relish the snail slime moments.

Select the timer icon in the bottom left-hand corner of the screen. A menu will appear with three options (minutes, hours, days). Underneath is an option to slide the number of frames taken. A frame is another name for the device taking an image. Increasing the number means that more images will be taken over that minute, hour or day. Press 'OK', then mount and leave the tablet so it won't be knocked or touched.

You could use this technique to teach how shadows are formed, how an assembly full of children is choreographed, or even the happenings of a normal school day.

 Movie introduction opening scene

Use the app to create an animated sequence to introduce the children to a film company they are going to set up. Play the children a number of introductions from age-appropriate children's

DVDs. Ask the children to identify how they may sell their ideas to the company who is producing the film.

As an alternative to DVDs, the iMovie app (https://itunes.apple.com/gb/app/imovie/id377298193?mt=8) has similar introductions when creating iMovie Trailers.

Navigate to the project tab and press the '+' button. There are two options – movie or trailer (the movie option will allow you to create a film from scratch whilst the trailer option will provide a scaffold and tell you the type of shot required and for how long a recorded piece of film is needed).

Select the 'New trailer' option. Once this option is selected then you are able to select sample trailers and preview them. The first few seconds are needed so the children can gain an overview of the company introduction. Ask the children to identify the common features a company introduction has at the beginning of a film. Ask the children to create a company name and then to produce their animated sequence for the beginning of their film. After animating, as an extension, the children can export the animation and add music to create their finished title sequence.

 ## Animating scientific concepts

Use 2D/3D models, shapes and figures to animate a science concept. Can the children describe through animation the sequence of food chains, how a house is built of different materials or the sequence of the water cycle? Export the finished animation to the camera roll so it can be imported into a video production app such as iMovie or Explain Everything (see Chapter 7).

 ## Silent movies

Create an animation to depict a story written during the times of silent movies. Silent movies produce an interesting opportunity to record a flashback from the past applying a special effect to give it that aged look.

Create the animation in I Can Animate and then export the movie to the camera roll, so it is in a video format. Using the iMovie app, begin a new project and then import the video into the timeline by pressing the content library icon (the film roll and musical note). Select the clip and then press the down arrow. Once the film clip is on the timeline, press on the clip so it is highlighted yellow. A separate set of options (cut, speed, sound, titles and colour) will appear.

There are two options to produce the effect for silent films: B&W (black and white) and the silent era. The silent era effect will also place the fading film lines down the screen. Press on the effect you wish and the effect will be applied. Once the film and the effects are complete, import a sound clip into your timeline to complete the project.

Importing background music

First locate a piece of music that could be used as background music for your movie. You could use the instruments using the Garageband app (https://itunes.apple.com/gb/app/garageband/id408709785?mt=8) or alternatively you can purchase a clip for student projects on the AudioNetwork website (www.audionetwork.com). This is a professional site many of the major television companies use to accompany their programmes. Browse by musical styles, mood, instrumentation or production genre. There are at least one hundred silent movie background tracks to use (Home > Production Genre > Film Styles > Silent Movies).

The quickest way to insert audio is to either attach the sound file to an email and email it back to yourself or upload it to a cloud storage service such as Dropbox. Once the sound file is pressed it will load and then the 'Share' button will appear somewhere on the screen.

If in Dropbox and using an iPad, press the 'Share' button and then select the 'Open in ... [another app]' option. Then scroll through the different apps until the 'Copy to iMovie' option appears. *Note, in order to see the 'Copy to iMovie' option, you must have iMovie installed.* It will either open up in a new movie project or ask you to select the project you would like to import the music into. The music will then be imported into the project.

The same process is true for opening up a sound file from the email on an Android tablet. Open the file and press 'Share'. However, instead of needing to select the 'Open in another app' option it will display the different apps so you can go through repeating the stages outlined above.

Once imported, the sound clips will be available to use for future projects by clicking on the content library icon (the film roll and musical note) then selecting the 'Audio' option. There is an option labelled 'Imported' where you are able to select from a list.

Adding narration and sound effects to an animated piece

This process is similar to the silent movie project. Create the animation in I Can Animate and then export the movie to the camera roll so it is in a video format. Using the iMovie app, begin a new project and then import the video into the timeline by pressing on the content library icon (the film roll and musical note). Select the clip and then press the down arrow. Once the film clip is on the timeline, return to the project's content library and select the 'Audio' option. There is a separate menu for sound effects; these can be previewed by pressing on the sound effect and pressing the play button. To insert the sound effect into your project, press the down arrow in the same way you added video to your timeline.

When you return to the timeline project screen, there are three further options displayed in the bottom right-hand corner – camera, microphone and project settings. The camera option allows you to take a photograph or video and add it to the project. The 'project settings' cog allows you to quickly change the overall colour filter or theme of the iMovie project, as well as being able to fine-tune certain elements of the project. The microphone in the middle of these options will produce the sound recorder. (If the message to allow access to the microphone appears then press 'Allow'.) The recorder will show the sound level so the children will know if they are talking too loudly; good to be green is the goal! Press 'Record' and the recorder will count down loudly from three. Record the narration and then press 'Stop'. You are presented with options so you can:

- retake the audio if you made a mistake;
- review the audio to check you are happy with the result, or
- accept the narration and then it is dropped down onto your timeline.

PUPPET PALS

Puppet Pals provides a stage on which characters can be manipulated across a stage scene. There are a core band of characters available to download and use. Ensure that you download the Director's Pass version (https://itunes.apple.com/gb/app/puppet-pals-hd-directors-pass/id462134755?mt=8). There is no difference between the free version and Director's Pass as they have the same content (cartoon characters). However, the Director's Pass has all the content unlocked whilst in the free version you have to pay to unlock the content through the app, which can be tiresome if a school has multiple devices.

⊗ Tell me a story

The simple use of Puppet Pals is to tell a story through the characters. The app guides you through the process. The first step is to select the characters you will manipulate on and off the stage. You can select up to eight characters (actors) by pressing on them and then selecting 'Next'. Then select a background. You can select up to five backgrounds. These appear to the right of the stage as curtain pulleys. When you press on each one, it will bring down the next backdrop in the same way the scene changes during a theatre production. The final screen is the stage.

Move the characters to the side and then press the red record button. Only characters within the background will be recorded.

Create a story using your characters, moving them on and off the screen whilst narrating your story. It is useful to have a story map or a script to support the children as they read.

Once the stop button is pressed then you have the option to play back the narrated story or to save it by entering a file name. Saved shows are saved under that heading on the front menu screen. From here you can export the show to the camera roll so it can be used in different mobile applications.

Step back in time

There is an additional feature when inserting characters and backgrounds and that is to add your own actors and backgrounds. Select the 'Add actor from photo' option and either use the camera to take a photograph of one of the children in your class or use a photograph already on the camera roll. Once selected, you will be prompted to cut out the character by drawing a line around them and then selecting 'Accept'. The same technique is used when adding your own background from your photographs.

Ask the children to work with a partner to take a photograph of themselves. In the camera roll, edit the image to make them black and white. Add and then cut out the chosen character and add to Puppet Pals. This is a useful activity for bringing history to life; children can source backgrounds in history books, for example a scene from World War II when children were evacuated and add in themselves. The children can then narrate what it was like to be an evacuee from the point of view of themselves in the newly created historic scene.

In the day of a bee

Another app to explore is the Toontastic app. This app provides a traditional story structure; however, you could delete unwanted parts and only use one of the structures. Toontastic is great for 2D animation and has a vast number of different characters to use. When the app is loaded, you progress through a linear method of content creation selecting your background, then selecting your characters (toys) before recording your narration. At the end, you can export the finished story to the camera roll (and share as a video with friends).

Draw a background of a dissected flower during part of your Science lesson. On the next screen when it prompts for a character, draw a bee. Then when it comes to recording the narration, narrate the process of pollination from a bee's perspective. Remember to add a note on the current bee situation and use the activity as an opportunity to raise children's awareness of environmental issues.

 Tour the classroom

Add characters and photographs from around your school. Combine these together to produce a tour of your school for prospective students as a transition project. As you narrate, include 'real' tips about getting used to the school and all the unofficial rules everyone should know such as what happens when there's a birthday in the school.

OTHER APPS

Brushes
Paper
ArtRage
Foldify

REFERENCES

Corbett, P. (2006). *Bumper Book of Story Telling into Writing at Key Stage 1*. Melksham: Clown Publishing.

Corbett, P. (2007). *Bumper Book of Story Telling into Writing at Key Stage 2*. Melksham: Clown Publishing.

CHAPTER 12

Welcome to our digital museum

Applications		
Camera app	free	
Class Dropbox account	free	
SuperPhoto	free	iPhone and iPad/Android
Snapseed	free	iPhone and iPad/Android
Adobe Lightroom	free	iPhone and iPad/Android
Molodiv	free	iPhone and iPad/Android
Book Creator	paid	iPhone and iPad/Android
QR code	free	iPhone and iPad/Android
Mobile Podcaster	paid	iPhone and iPad
Opinion Podcasts	free	iPhone and iPad
Spreaker	free	iPhone and iPad/Android
Do Ink	paid	iPhone and iPad

MULTIPLE APP PROJECTS

This chapter incorporates a number of different activities and apps. Some activities are focused entirely on apps, whilst others use the mobile device in conjunction with other physical resources.

Life in a museum is a very exciting place to explore as a young person. This chapter could be used to build classwork around a school visit to a museum or may be used as a framework to support a fictional museum you create as a class. So in this section, a number of ideas, activities and apps are presented to support the building of a digital museum. A topic like this provides an ideal opportunity once completed to extend an invitation to the wider school community so they can come and look around and experience the work you have built as a class. The premise of this activity stems from the final task, which is to invite parents and other adults to come and attend the opening of the museum. Museums can have different interests and different topics. They connect the subjects of literacy, arts and technology in order to present work.

ACTIVITIES

Creating a digital museum

Design and create a digital museum with artefacts you have made. Invite your parents and the wider school community after school to visit the museum.

Resources needed for this project

Camera app
Class Dropbox account
SuperPhoto
Snapseed
Adobe Lightroom
Molodiv
Book Creator
QR code
Mobile Podcaster
Opinion Podcasts
Spreaker
Do Ink

Photographing the artefact

Museums need objects to display, whether they are paintings or physical objects. As a class, decide on the artefacts that you're going to exhibit to your public. You may choose to create these in an Art lesson; provide children with an amount of clay they can fashion into a pot, a piece of jewellery or a different artefact which would have been used in a given history period. Alternatively, it could be an object that has just been discovered, and the children have to make the object out of papier-mâché and decide on both its use and on the story of how/where it was found. Activities like this provide meaningful cross-curricular opportunities; in this example the key subjects would be Art and English.

Once the object is made, use a camera tool to photograph it. Then use photo-editing apps such as SuperPhoto, Snapseed or Adobe Lightroom (to add effects to the photographs). Finally, export the photograph back to the camera roll before opening it in Molodiv. Molodiv is an app that allows you to create collages and magazine front covers; it also allows the user to edit photographs with different effects and then save these back to the camera roll. Collect these images into a shared or collaborative document for children to access at a later time.

✍ Writing a description of your artefact

Whilst not a mobile app, use an internet browser on the mobile device to access PrimaryPad (http://primarypad.com). This is a very quick and easy tool to use if you want your class to collaborate on a shared writing task, or for them to collect ideas or share their thoughts. In the top right-hand corner of the website, there is an option to 'Create pad'. Select this option and a unique URL is generated such as http://free.primarypad.com/p/QGudmbkDCH. Share this link with the children, either by creating it into a QR code (see Chapter 4) or place it in a shared area that all mobile devices can access. A similar result is also achievable with a shared Google Document accessed through the GoogleDocs app.

Ask the children to write a description of their artefact in the PrimaryPad. To make it easier, type all the children's names into the pad, leaving a line space between each name, so they know where to type.

🚻 Create a welcome to the museum brochure

Using Book Creator (see Chapter 6), ask the children to create a brochure which parents will download at certain key places as they tour the museum. The finished brochure will be attached to a QR code.

Divide your class into table groups; each table group will be responsible for setting up a 'zone' of the museum. As the parents walk around, one of the group members will present a QR code which is then scanned and leads to a mini brochure being loaded on to their mobile device.

1. Begin by creating a new book in a portrait page orientation. Ask the children to create their guide to their zone ensuring that they include:

    i.   A welcome message from the group.
    ii. Photographs of the exhibits their guests will see and the order to see the exhibits in.
    iii. A description of how the collection ties together as well as extra information for the reader, for example, where the artefact was found.

2. Once the children have finished, export each guide as a PDF.
3. You will need a URL (website) link to where each of the documents have been stored. You could create a class Dropbox account (www.dropbox.com) where you can then copy the document link by clicking the 'Share' button and copying the link which is then created. Or export the books from Book Creator as a PDF file, which can then be embedded into separate blog posts (if you have a class blog), so that each group has a separate URL link for their brochure guide.
4. With these links, create a QR code for each of the guides. Then copy them into a Word document and print off each of the codes, adding titles and group information as you go. As each visitor walks around the museum and when they reach a new zone of the museum, they can scan the QR code and are then presented with the group's brochure explaining the zone.

Creating an audio tour of the museum

Produce an audio tour for people as they walk around the museum. Whilst there are some apps that allow you to record voice, there are some podcasting apps that allow the user to add a description or photograph; others allow you to add sound effects, creating a more professional appearance. Two of the simpler apps children can use are Mobile Podcaster and Opinion.

- *Mobile Podcaster* is a basic recorder. At the bottom of the screen are three simple controls. Press the record button and the recorder instantly begins the podcasting. Press the stop button and the new recording appears. Pressing on the recording will play the podcast from the start. There is an 'i' option at the end of the recording, which allows description to be added but it is also possible to share and upload the audio track to a WordPress site, send by email or open it in another app.
- *Opinion* is another simple app to use, but what is nice about the way this app works is that it visually shows the chunks of colourful sound recording as well as providing the option to rearrange the sections, or to cut out unwanted parts of the recording if mistakes are made. Music can also be imported so children can add introduction music or their own musical compositions. There is a ten-minute maximum time length allowed without unlocking the app, which provides ample space.

For a more advanced app, Spreaker allows you to add different sound effects in real time as you record your podcast, such as applause, laughter and suspense music. Although an advanced app, the only drawback is that the finished recording has to be uploaded to the Spreaker platform. There are ways of getting around this by visiting the platform through a desktop computer and previewing the track, where a download button is presented underneath the track. Pressing this will download the track as an mp3.

Save the downloaded mp3s into a Dropbox folder, create a QR code and then the parents or other visitors can click through and listen to the tracks one by one, as they navigate round the museum.

⊗ Illustrated map of the whole museum

Draw an aerial view of the classroom on to a large piece of sugar paper. Invite the children to draw on the location of their artefact in the classroom and what it looks like looking down on the object. As soon as the map is complete, use the camera to take a photograph of the map. Parents and invited guests will use this image as they tour around the museum. Use Chirp (https://itunes.apple.com/gb/app/chirp/id529469280?mt=8) to pass the image to visitors' phones as they enter the museum. Chirp uses sound to transfer information from one device to another. Any device with a speaker or microphone can send and receive data using the app. The other person needs to have the Chirp app, so parents could either have the app downloaded or use the school mobile devices whilst in the museum.

The app is simple in design. As the app loads, press the '+' button. From here you are able to attach an image from the camera roll, write a text note, send a website URL, film a video or send a picture taken with the camera app. Select your option and find or enter the desired information. Once attached, press the yellow Chirp button which will send the sound signal ready for other devices with Chirp open to receive.

🔆 Video introduction using green screen

Every good museum needs a video introduction that showcases what visitors can expect as they tour around the museum. As part of an English activity, write a class script for the opening of the video welcoming parents and invited guests to the museum. Ensure that every child in the class has something to say during the film. If the artefacts are fictitious, you could describe how they were discovered, for example, did they belong to a king or queen from past times? Were they discovered by a famous explorer, and what perhaps were the circumstances of the discovery? Did a battle on water take place and the ship was sunk and then 50 years later the artefacts were once again discovered?

Film short videos of the artefacts and then the children against the green screen reading their sections of the script created as a class. Load the Do Ink app and begin a new project by clicking the '+' button and selecting 'Create a new project'. When the project loads, insert the videos and images of the artefacts on the bottom line by pressing the '+' to the right of the line. Select the source (video and image) then repeat the same process on the second timeline, inserting the green screen video of the children talking about their artefacts. Use the chroma background tools to fine-tune the green screen out to reveal the artefacts below.

⊗ Create a gift shop

Although not an activity that involves a mobile device, the final activity in a multiple app project could be to open a gift shop with items produced during Design Technology lessons, or with cakes and biscuits brought in from home. This could be as a result of an activity the PTA organises, such as Christmas decorations or other craft activities. After a successful sale, and when all the costs are accounted for, the class can then decide what to do with the profits and whether to purchase something for the school or donate to different local charities.

CHAPTER 13
Superheroes

Applications		
Book Creator	free (paid version available)	iPhone/iPad/Android
Comic Life	free	iPhone/iPad/Android
Toontastic	free	iPhone/iPad
ArtRage	paid	iPhone/iPad/Android
Tayasui Sketches	free	iPhone/iPad/Android
Paper	free	iPhone/iPad
Procreate	paid	iPhone/iPad
ClassFlow	free	iPhone/iPad/Android
Word Wizard	paid (free on Android)	iPhone/iPad/Android
Foldify	paid	iPhone/iPad/Android

CROSS-CURRICULAR LEARNING

Is it a bird? Is it a plane? Is there an app for that?

When it comes to cross-curricular learning, there are a number of apps that can be used in combination to support a topic such as this one focused on superheroes. With the popularity of films such as The Incredibles, Superman, The Avengers, Wonder Woman, Batman and Spiderman, there is a wide range of superheroes, and indeed villains, for children to identify with and choose from. The topic of superheroes creates a fantasy world for children to explore; in addition to thinking about their superhero, they have to think about the world they inhabit, fictional or otherwise, as well as considering the traditional plot of good versus evil.

> **The task**
>
> *Design and create the world of a superhero*
>
> You will need to create a superhero, considering any superpowers, special vehicles, weapons or other tricks they may have up their sleeve. Use multiple applications to tell their story and answer the question: will the force of good triumph over evil?
>
> Use any of the apps outlined above for this project.

ACTIVITIES

 Creating a superhero story

The topic of superheroes lends itself to the creation of a text narrative as well as through the more traditional comic strip format. Use a familiar app such as Book Creator or Comic Life to make a comic about a superhero; both these apps allow the user to create original comic strips, as well as being able to personalise the template through the insertion of speech bubbles, text and onomatopoeic words, all of which can be applied directly within the app.

To generate ideas, host a **Superheroes Party** and invite the children to dress up as their chosen hero. As a party icebreaker, ask the children to walk around and when you say 'stop', the children will need to introduce themselves to the closest superhero and find out a little more about them, for example their name, the land they grew up in, the type(s) of superpowers they have and any other super quality they can share. To extend the idea, you could ask the children to mime the superpower to see if their partner can guess what it is.

 Toontastic: your superhero story

Another way to create a superhero story is to explore the use of the Toontastic app.

Begin by creating a new cartoon. The children are presented with the traditional story arc, which they may be familiar with: the opening or background *(the set up), the conflict, the challenge, the climax* and finally *the resolution.* An audio description accompanies each of the story arc elements as they are selected. The cartoon can be personalised by editing and moving scenes using a green paintbrush and a red delete dustbin. To delete a scene, simply press on the red delete dustbin. Further scenes can be added by selecting the 'Add scenes' option in the bottom left-hand corner. Pressing the green paintbrush reveals the setting options. Scroll to the right to reveal template backgrounds, or scroll to the left to paint your own scene, which might be the superhero's lair or another background of choice.

Next, the exciting part! Scroll to the right and you will discover a wealth of different characters whose legs and arms move as you move around the screen. You can select any number of different characters to play a part in your story.

Scroll to the left, and there are some special toys called **ProtoToys**. These actors feel like the normal characters you use to animate with within the app, however, there is one difference: the ProtoToys allow you to draw on each of the toy's different parts. For example, the **SuperProto** is an outline of a blank superhero; the hair, head, body, arms and legs are presented as silhouettes and the painting tray at the bottom of the screen allows you to draw each body part to create your own superhero.

The next step is to click on the green tick and assemble the SuperProto body parts and then you have created your own superhero character to use in the scene. There are also ProtoToys for people, fast cars, rockets, helicopters, monster trucks and animals, which provide the children with a whole scope of options to create their very own superhero cartoon.

Next, press 'Start' to progress to the animating stage, which works in a similar way to Puppet Pals (see Chapter 11). As the characters move across the screen, they can speak the chosen dialogue at the same time; there is also the possibility to add different types of background music and movie titles. To finish, press the stop option before exporting the finished movie to the camera roll.

🗨 Designing a superhero and their logo

Ask the children to draw their superhero and logo either using paper or using drawing apps such as ArtRage, Tayasui Sketches, Paper or Procreate. Look for on-screen inspiration, for example the British Council has a feature on superheroes (http://learn englishkids.britishcouncil.org/en/make-your-own/style-hero), and build up a bank of different superheroes. The children can then select the different features they would like to include for their hero. Encourage the children to consider the detail of their character; for example, can their clothing be adapted in some way? What might look like ordinary sunglasses may in fact be hiding a special power. Use the art apps to draw an accompanying costume logo of both the hero and the villain – think of the big **S** for Superman, or the double **W** found on Wonder Woman's outfit. Export the images to the camera roll to use in future projects.

🍽 Designing an imaginary land for the superheroes

Use one of the painting apps suggested in the previous activity, and ask the children to design or sketch an imaginary land for their superhero. Invite the children to think about:

- Where does their superhero live?
- Do they live on the ground or underground?
- Do they live in a town or in a completely fictional fantasy land?
- What do they live in? A volcano? A tree house? An ordinary house?
- Do they have hidden stores of weapons?
- Do they have fellow partners in crime who also live in their land?

When the children have finished designing their land, ask them to export their finished painting to the camera roll. Then, using Book Creator (see Chapter 6), they can make a one-page landscape book of their image, which can then be airdropped to the teacher's iPad, ready to combine all the books together to create one class book of superhero settings.

⊗ Costume design

Superheroes need a distinctive costume and objects within their imaginary world. The Foldify app allows the user to select a generic template that can then be painted and customised. Once created, the children can print off the net of their creation and fold it together to make their superhero or object. This activity provides wonderful links with Mathematics, as children learn about 3D shapes and how they are made up of a set of 2D shapes, represented as a net. Additional features like brushes, colours, cartoon stamps and facial features are also included. As the children draw and paint, their finished product is shown in real time. Once completed, the children can send the file wirelessly to a printer or email a PDF of the net for manual printing. A good superhero example can be found on the Foldify website (www.foldifyapp.com).

⚲ Designing a superhero poster using ClassFlow

Having decided on their superhero, his/her peculiar characteristics and designed their own logo and costume, the next task is for the children to create a wanted poster for their superhero.

Explore the use of Promethean's ClassFlow (www.classflow.co. uk) to encourage task collaboration. You will need to activate a free teacher's account, which will allow you to create **cards** you can send to the children's devices. ClassFlow allows multiple devices with an internet connection (tablets, mobile phones and computers) to connect to the class interactive whiteboard, regardless of the type of board. There are a number of different options, but one of the most exciting is the ability to ask questions and elicit responses from the children, including the ability to send what is called a **creative poll**. This provides the children with a blank card and a set of tools such as pens, text, shapes and lines and, more importantly, the ability to take an image using the mobile's camera so the children can send a real image of their work in front of them.

Setting up a ClassFlow lesson

Begin by signing into ClassFlow (www.classflow.co.uk) to build a lesson. Click on '**My resources**' and then '**New**' followed by the '**New lesson**' option. You can design multiple cards with information and images using the tools that load in the top left and right of the screen. This task uses the tool that allows you to interact with the children by eliciting their responses using the electronic devices.

Click the name of your presentation and rename the heading that is already there, then click '**Present**'. If you have not already set up your class, select an 'Ad hoc session (no class)', which still allows the children to connect to the lesson.

Ask the children to go to an internet browser and go to www.classflow.co.uk/student and select the '**Join a class**' option on the login screen.

Connect your class to the lesson by pressing the '**Connect Student**' icon in the top right-hand corner displaying the number. This then displays a code for the children to connect to the lesson you are delivering. The children type in the code and their device is connected to the session. They will see a *holding screen* in between the time of you sending response cards, and the number of devices will increase as more children connect to the lesson. The children need to enter their name and press '**Join anyway**' to gain access to the lesson.

Once all the children are connected, select the poll option from the toolbar on the right-hand side and then select '**Text response**'.

To begin the activity, ask the children to think of a word or phrase to describe a specific quality of their superhero (strong, able to swim underwater, can transform any object by saying the phrase ...). Select the '**Start Poll**' option, then press on '**Word Seed**', which will begin the poll. Ask the children to choose one good idea and type it into the box provided before clicking the '**Submit**' button. Once all the children have submitted their ideas, the responses will be grouped together under the 'Assessment and Poll Responses' button at the top of the screen. Take a screenshot of the screen displaying the responses for the children to respond to later on.

Move on to the next blank page and run the poll again, and this time, ask the children to name three to five items a superhero would own (e.g., rocket boots, cape of invisibility, cat ears, Google glasses, thunder gloves, etc.). Ask the children to include at least one animal quality, for example the ability to run like a leopard. Tell the children to type these into one long line, separating the items with commas before pressing the 'Submit' button. Remember to take a screenshot of the responses.

Finally, repeat the process again, but for this task, the children need to create four different superhero names, one for a man, one for a woman, one for a boy and one for a girl. This preparation work then leads to the next suggested activity: 'Superhero mashup'.

Superhero mashup

Place a number of small sticky notes and pens on the children's tables. Log into ClassFlow and click on the 'My Resources' tab at the top of the screen. You will see the superhero lesson you were working on. Click on this lesson and then select 'Edit Lesson', which will transfer you to the Lesson Builder. Select '+Insert' from the menu, which will take you to 'My Resources'. From here, select 'Upload New Resources' and select one of the screenshots from the previous activity, then press 'Upload'. Once the process is complete, select 'Insert in New Card'. Repeat the process for each of the screenshots then exit the Lesson Builder. Finally, press 'Deliver' to run the lesson. Share each of the slides/cards with the children's devices. As a group, ask the children to write down six of their favourite suggestions from the board and write them on to separate sticky notes. Once they have finished choosing, they should have 18 different sticky notes:

- 6 × qualities of a superhero
- 6 × items a superhero would own
- 6 × superhero names

The next step is for the children to work in a group to create their own collaborative group superhero. Ask the children to number each set of sticky notes from one to six and give each group a dice and a large piece of paper. Ask the children to roll the dice and whichever number is rolled, the children take that sticky note and stick it onto the larger piece of paper. They will need to roll three times for the qualities of a superhero, three times for the items a superhero would have and once for the superhero's name.

Once the children have their seven sticky notes, challenge the children to draw and create their group superhero. Towards the end of the task, send the creative card option to the children's devices by clicking the poll option and then the '**Creative**' option from the list. Using the camera, each group takes a photograph of their finished group superhero and uses the text and pen tools to annotate the photograph with the name and special features of their hero. Once finished, the children press the '**Submit**' arrow in the top right-hand corner. Once all the children have submitted their superhero press the '**Stop**' button to end the poll (found on the right-hand side).

In the title bar, a square 'View poll results' button is provided. Click on this to reveal all the submitted responses, which will appear along the bottom with the children's names. Pressing on the image will display the cards in a larger format and a pen is provided so you can annotate on top of the card. When you are ready you can also add the card back into the lesson to use at a later stage. The submitted poll responses are also stored, and the same button reveals the lesson's results and assessment data. Once the card is added to the lesson, it can be used and sent to the children's devices in the same way as the other cards used within the ClassFlow lesson. Further support videos are also available on the ClassFlow YouTube channel (https://www.youtube.com/user/MyClassFlow).

♟ Writing a superhero pledge

After completing the sketch of the superhero, the children will need to take a picture and save it to the camera roll. Using the Typic or Typic Kids app, ask them to insert the photograph of their superhero and write a pledge to the rest of the world about the things they will strive to achieve. For example:

I, Spadeboy, solemnly undertake this pledge to save the land of Chocoville from the evil Professor R.T. Fact and Dr Bell. Whenever something happens I will respond, be prepared to fight to save others who are weaker than I and be a force for good.

SPADEBOY

Once in the app, the children need to insert the photograph from their camera roll and apply effects and text (by swiping right to left) until the picture pledge is completed.

Spellcheck using Word Wizard

Use the moveable alphabet feature of Word Wizard to encourage the children to check the spelling of unfamiliar words. When drafting ideas for their pledges, and they are unsure of a word, ask the children to underline the spelling with a dotted line, which will avoid limiting the flow of their writing. Tell the children they will need to spellcheck their writing using Word Wizard.

At the editing stage of the writing process, load the Word Wizard app and ask the child (or scribe for the group) to look at the dotted, underlined spelling and try to spell it out by dragging the letter tiles letter by letter. As each letter is placed on the board the app will sound them out. If two tiles are placed next to each other, the blended letters will be sounded out. Children can then check their spellings and make any necessary corrections. The sweeping brush then clears the entire board ready to restart with the next spelling. It is worth noting that by clicking the settings cog, there is the possibility to change the accent of the voice from American to English.

OTHER APPS

Brushes
Paper
ArtRage
Foldify

CHAPTER 14
Crime scene investigations

Applications		
WordPress	free	website or blog
Camera app	free	
Skitch	free	iPad/iPhone/Android
Trello	free	iPad/iPhone/Android
iMovie	free	iPad/iPhone
TouchCast Studio	free	iPad/iPhone
Vintage Design	paid	iPad/iPhone
Lifecards	paid	iPad/iPhone
Postale	paid	iPad/iPhone/Android
Moldiv	free	iPad/iPhone/Android
Google Earth	free	iPad/iPhone/Android
Apple Maps	free	iPad/iPhone
Barefoot World Atlas	paid	iPad/iPhone/Android
Tellagami	free	iPad/iPhone/Android

This topic draws its inspiration from the American Christmas tradition of the *Elf of the Shelf*. This special elf has been sent by Santa Claus to help manage the *naughty* and *nice* lists. The idea is that each family adopts an elf and names her. The elf is then awarded with a special magical power, which gives her the ability to fly to the North Pole each night to tell Father Christmas about all of the day's adventures. Each morning, the elf returns to the family and greets the children from an unexpected place; sometimes the elf is not where the children think she is going to be, so the first task is to find her and see what mischief she's been up to. This provides adults with an opportunity to set up little scenarios that the children can discover.

There are two simple rules. First, the elf cannot be touched; the magic is very fragile and if the elf is touched, she may lose the magic and be unable to fly back to the North Pole. Second, the elf cannot speak or move whilst anyone is awake, so they remain still but watch and listen to what is going on.

To use the same idea but in the classroom, it is necessary to change some of the details. There is still an elf, but each night she flies back to the North Pole via the headteacher. When the elf returns to the classroom in the middle of the night, she parties hard with the class mascot until the children return at the start of the school day. The elf and the class mascot become the best of friends, with the elf introducing the class mascot to a new place of interest on the way home from the North Pole.

ACTIVITIES

 Blogging

You will need to have a selected class mascot from the beginning of the year (you're likely to run this activity during December). Send the mascot home to a different child each evening and remember that he needs to take his own diary ready to write in the activities that he gets up to with the child and their parents (some adult help may be required).

Use the WordPress app to collect this information. Once your free blog is linked with the app, you can sign in before being presented with a number of options, such as the ability to create a post. Set up an additional user/login so that parents can also become authors on the blog. They will need to have downloaded the app and have the login details. For security reasons, you can also change the password each time the mascot goes to a home. From the app, the parent can create a post and upload photographs of the class mascot and his various activities, for example having supper, cleaning his teeth, or going to Brownies or Cubs. You may wish to include some instructions for creating a blog in a home/school mascot book.

The task

HELP!!!

Your class mascot needs your help! Over the past half term, the Elf has been best friends with our class mascot. However, late last night, the Evil Travelling Iron Man (E-TIM) stole both the Elf and our class mascot. Confident that you won't catch him, he has left a ransom note saying that he aims to hide Elf and the mascot in different parts of the world, and he won't return them until you guess the locations the E-TIM has taken them to.

Each morning, you will receive a clue from E-TIM that you will need to follow. This may be a photograph from travel agents' brochures, or different clues of writings, letters, etc. All that he will give you is a class passport, and each time you guess the correct location, you will receive a stamp or sticker. Only when all the locations are guessed, will your mascot be returned. In order to follow your journey and track your progress, you will need to report back in a journalistic way as each of the events unfolds in the classroom. The better your reporting, the more clues E-TIM will leave when he visits at night time.

☁ Capturing the crime scene

Set up a crime scene in the classroom for the children to explore: leave behind the evidence of where Elf and the mascot have been taken as they were eating their dinner. Left behind is a letter from E-TIM explaining that he has taken the pair and will hide them in various places around the world. In order to be safely returned, the children will have to work out where they have been hidden using clues taken from the postcards he will send them.

To set the scene, include:

- cordoning off the area with tape (police tape if you can source it);
- torn out pieces of a travel brochure scattered around the scene;

- a map with co-ordinates providing clues to the first location in the world where Elf and mascot may be hiding;
- anything else that captures your teacher's imagination!

You can either set up one very large scene for the children to work in groups to analyse, or you can spread the information around the whole of the classroom to create mini-satellite scenes.

Some tips and resources online

There are a couple of places for resources and inspiration on how to turn your classroom into a forensic lab:

www.theguardian.com/teacher-network/teacher-blog/2013/mar/27/ forensic-science-csi-teaching-tips-classroom

http://stem-works.com/subjects/10-crime-scene-investigation/ activities

http://education.scholastic.co.uk/content/9794

Using the camera tool, ask the children to take photographs of the scene in order to remind them of the events that have occurred. Use Skitch to annotate the photographs with any detail they think looks suspicious.

Explain to the class they will need to collect their initial thoughts about the crime and use the photographs as evidence. Use the Trello app (https://trello.com/platforms) and create a **board** called 'Crime Scene Investigations'.

Three **cards** will appear, and by tapping on the heading of each card it can be easily renamed so children know where to put their work. Create a list for each group and press '**Add list**' to add additional lists to make a group. In the top right-hand corner, the three dots allow you to add members so they can contribute to the board. Press '**Add member**' and add the school email address shared by the class iPads. Each iPad user will then be able to add their thoughts and take notes on the crime scene they are investigating. Use suggested questions like:

- What will they need to follow up on?
- What looks suspicious?

By pressing the cards, the children can add additional thoughts in the description box, as well as add their photographs as attachments.

👤 I'll get right to that, Chief

The Chief of Police has asked you to feed back to her about the incident that has happened in your school. She is away travelling at the moment, and so she needs you to record your report and send it to her so she can assess the progress of the investigation. She needs to see what you have found out, so remember to show her your evidence. For this activity, the children will create a filmed news report. Ask the children to draft their script before filming the report and then film the finished news report using the camera app. Take on the role of a news reporter, and during the filming sit to the right of the screen in much the same way as you might see a real news reporter on the television.

Convert all your photographs into one long movie (you will be able to cut out the exact sections you wish to keep at a later stage). Start by beginning a new iMovie project that needs to be separate from your report to the police chief project. Add all the photographs taken for the timeline by pressing on the photo option and then navigating to the correct photographs.

The 'Ken Burns' zooming effect will automatically be turned on, but remove this effect by pressing on the photograph in the timeline and looking at the larger picture displayed. At the bottom right-hand corner, you will be presented with a number of options. Press on the 'Ken Burns Enabled' icon, which will disable this feature. Repeat for all the photographs inserted on the timeline, before clicking '**Done**' and export the video back to the camera roll by clicking the share option and then '**Save video**'.

Finally, combine both the video containing the photographs and the report video. Begin by loading the report video. Press on '**Video**' from the video, photos and audio options in order to add the video you have just created. Locate and press on the video. Two yellow hands will appear so you can trim the clip. Find the exact image you need and three options will appear – an option to add that clip to the timeline; to play the selected clip to check you have the correct section and then three dots to display more options. Select **More options** and then locate the 'picture-in-picture' option (the fourth option along). This shoots the video down to the timeline but places it on top of the main video. The video is displayed in a box in the top left-hand corner of the main movie.

Newspaper article

This is a similar activity to the one above; however, instead of sending the video back to the police chief, the children need to create a news report to explain what has happened. If the class has a Twitter feed, they can post updates of the investigation by practising how to tweet. This activity also provides a useful opportunity to reflect on the digital citizenship implications of using social media tools as a whole class.

Use TouchCast to produce an interactive broadcast. The TouchCast app allows you to record a video, as well as being able to place interactive elements on the screen at the same time, e.g., a Twitter feed, or an interactive webpage using video, images or a file. There are also some pre-set backgrounds such as the NEWS STUDIO that you can place directly in the environment. Press the '**Record**' button and record your news story.

Create a WANTED poster

Use one of the painting apps (see Chapter 9) to sketch an image of the E-TIM (Evil Travelling IronMan). Save the image to the camera roll and use a poster app such as Vintage Design to design a wanted poster. There are some great backgrounds to be used under the wood background category. Alternatively, use a collage or a word processor app to create your wanted poster.

Postcards from the E-TIM

Use the Lifecards app or the Postale app to create postcards containing the clues left by E-TIM about where he has taken Elf and the class mascot. You could create a collage for the front of the postcard using Moldiv. The children could then use topic books and an atlas like the interactive Barefoot World Atlas to explore the countries and places E-TIM mentions.

☁ Reports from sightings

Use the Tellagami app, which allows friends to record messages of sightings of E-TIM, Elf and the class mascot. The app creates different types of characters that can be customised as well as the background. After this, a voice or typed message from the character can be attached to the Tellagami before using the tools on the mobile device. This allows you to play different characters without revealing your face, so hopefully the children won't guess it's you.

CHAPTER 15
Story making

Application

Book Creator (Free)

Subject possibilities

English, Art, Design Technology

Category

- Apple device (iPad/iPhone) – free (also a paid version)
- Android app – free

WHAT THE APP DOES

Similar to other applications that allow the user to become a published author, Book Creator is an engaging and easy way to combine text and photographs to tell stories. However, the stories can also be non-fiction, so the app is suitable to be used in a wide range of contexts, beyond only being used in an English lesson. One key advantage of the app is that it can be used to create multiple books and for them to be 'mashed' together; it also works very effectively when app smashing (a process of merging content across applications). It's easy to see where Book Creator can combine with Explain Everything (see Chapter 7), YouTube or Vimeo (for embedding video), and I Can Present (a script writing or teleprompt tool).

Our Story (see Chapter 6) works in a similar way, as it offers an innovative yet straightforward approach to storytelling or chronological retellings, through the use of photographs, text and audio. The Our Story app uses a simple format of a filmstrip for children to drag and drop photographs from the camera roll before adding their own text or audio. Navigation is uncomplicated and the menu of choices is kept to a minimum, enabling children to engage with the storytelling process, rather than being distracted by font decisions. See Chapter 6 for other creative activities with Our Story.

THE APP IN CONTEXT

Book Creator can be used across subjects and adapted to suit the skills of children in both key stages. The use of technology to support storytelling or retelling allows the imagination to consider possibilities within a visual and audio environment, rather than being restricted to creating and designing solely through text. There are opportunities for children to collaborate on projects, as they can work independently on projects by sharing their ideas, making decisions and meshing together the final project. Children in Years 5 and 6 are required to participate in discussions and debates within English, and to collaborate with others through the effective communication of their ideas. Whilst the focus of the project may be on a written output, Book Creator supports quality spoken language experiences.

ACTIVITIES

⊗ Creating a story book
1. Begin by selecting the 'New book' option in the top left-hand corner. From here you can select different sizes of books – portrait, square, landscape as well as the same orientations in comic strip style versions.

2. Use the 'Rory's Story Cubes' (https://itunes.apple.com/gb/app/rorys-story-cubes/id342808551?mt=8) to generate ideas for a story. By gently shaking the device, the nine story cubes are generated with an image on each one. The task is to create a story inspired by the use of the story cubes. They don't need to be used in order, but the challenge is to link all of the nine cubes in a story.

3. Once the new book is open, there are arrows on the left- and right-hand sides of the page to navigate through the book. Navigate to the second page and then press the '+' sign and press on 'Add text'. Write the first line of the story and then continue on each of the subsequent pages. When you get to the end of your last page the arrow will change into a '+' sign so you can add more pages until you have the required number of pages for your story.

4. To add an image, press on the '+' sign and either draw a picture with the pen or complete the artwork separately and add the illustrations by taking a photograph using the camera option under the '+' sign.

Customising content and adding interactivity

When you insert any of the content (text, photographs, sounds) on to the page, select the content, so the blue circles appear. You will then be able to resize the content by adjusting the corner. In the top-right corner of the screen is an 'i' **information** icon. When content is selected and the 'i' is pressed, various options will appear.

Function	Option
Shapes	Colour, shadow, border, layout
Image	Hyperlink to a website, layout
Text	Size, colour, alignment, effect, layout
Sound	Layout, ability to make the sound element invisible when the whole book is exported to iBooks

---

Interactive story/topic map

Provide an audio carousel of tasks for the children to work through in a lesson or over a week with the aim of creating an interactive story or a topic map. By adding an image, in this case a star, additional information is provided for the reader in the form of an **information hotspot**. The hotspots might provide clues about a character or additional instructions about where to head to next on the map.

1. Search for a free background through a web browser. Select a background that relates to a magical story or an image from a topic you are currently working on.
2. On the image, hold down your finger until a menu appears. Save the image to the camera roll by pressing '**Save image**'; this will allow you to import it into Book Creator.
3. Open a new **landscape** book in the Book Creator app.
4. Press the '+' to add item and then press '**Photos**'. Insert the photograph on to the cover. *Resize the image by dragging out the blue handles until the image covers the whole page.*
5. Press and hold down your finger on the image and a menu will appear where you can '**Lock**' the image so the image will not move.
6. Next, click on 'Add Item' and on the top right of the menu bar you'll find a '**Shapes**' icon. Select a star shape and add this to the map/image. Resize the shape and place it around the map/image.

    Each star acts as a hotspot or a tiny piece of information for the children to follow. By pressing on the star, a menu will appear with an option to '**Duplicate**' the shape; this action replicates the shape's size and proportions, saving you time without the hassle of resizing each individual shape.
7. Once the star shapes are dotted around the image/map, tap on each star and press to activate the menu. '**Lock**' each of the shapes in place.
8. On top of each star, record a sound (see box below).

Recording a sound

1. Press 'Add item' and then 'Record sound'. *A separate dialogue will appear with a round red record button.*

2. Record the sound. This could be an instruction, a piece of information about the topic, a sound clip sound or a question for the children to think about.

3, Press the 'Stop' button and a grey sound box will appear. The sound clip can then be dragged into the correct place. *Pressing in the middle of the sound clip plays the sound recording.*

 How to ... guides

During an instructional writing unit of work, you can demonstrate how to follow a simple recipe. For example, this could be linked to a World War II topic where the children are exploring how to make Woolton pie (full of vegetables) or an uncooked chocolate cake (the clue's in the name). A useful starting point is Birmingham Museum & Art Gallery for Kids (www.schoolsliaison.org.uk/ kids/siteactivities/warrecipe.pdf). Their school section (www. schoolsliaison.org.uk/2004/general/printables.htm) also provides a useful location for further resources.

Make a simple recipe in front of the children. As the activity progresses, ask the children to take photos of the key points as you create each step; one group member may need to jot down notes of the detail. At the end of the demonstration, each group can compare their photographs and can potentially swap using the **AirDrop** function.

Using AirDrop

AirDrop is a function whereby you can pass files from one Apple device to another Apple device. If your school subscribes to another device-sharing system (e.g., AirWatch), this function is enabled within that service and you don't need AirDrop.

1.   From the bottom of the screen, swipe a finger up from the bevelled edge to reveal the control centre.
2.   Ensure that the Bluetooth and wireless functions are toggled on (the two options sit beside each other).
3.   Beneath these options are two options – AirDrop and AirPlay. Press on the AirDrop option to reveal a second menu – '*Off – Contacts Only – Everyone*'. Ensure that the **Everyone** option is selected and then press on the screen outside the control centre to send it away.

To send a photograph to another device:

5.   Load the Photos app and navigate to a photograph you would like to send.
6.   Click the share option in the top-right corner (the square with the vertical up-arrow); this will then present a number of different places to share to. If other devices have AirDrop then the devices will appear at the top in a grey circle with the name of the iPad.
7.   Press on the device you wish to exchange the file with and it will send the recipient the file in the same way you would exchange playing cards, for example.

Once the children have all the photographs they need to recreate the recipe, and are sure they have noted down the main points, they can combine them into a visual recipe with instructions.

Begin a new book and combine the text and photos together, until the **How to guide** is complete.

🔍 Into the museum: smart 'digital' style

Creating a museum and asking the children to become the museum curator is a great way for them to demonstrate their knowledge of a topic they have been researching over a number of weeks.

1. As a class Art or History activity or as a piece of half-term homework, ask the children to make an artefact from the class topic. Explain to them they will exhibit their artefact in the class museum, but in addition, they will also be creating an audio factfile.
2. Using a new landscape book, ask the children to create a factfile or a presentation slide for their chosen subject area or artefact.
3. Select 'Add item' and use the camera to take two or three photographs of the artefact and place these on the page.
4. Use the 'Text' tool to provide a title for the object, and then insert some new text to write the museum description for people to read as they wander from artefact to artefact.
5. Next, ask the children to work on their own or in pairs to create an audio description for their artefact using a word processor to enlarge the font for the reader. Alternatively, they could use the I Can Present app (https://itunes.apple.com/gb/app/i-can-present/id632047471?mt=8).

I Can Present app

The app allows you to type or paste a script into the app and then use it as a teleprompter, if required, whilst making a recording at the same time. You can change font size, style and colour to make it comfortable to read.

I Can Present has three different presentation modes:

*   **Taking a video only.** This will record video using the rear- or the forward-facing camera.
*   **Script only.** This is the teleprompter mode, so that one child can hold up the iPad as a teleprompter and read the script out aloud as another person films the child speaking using another device.

> • **Video and script mode.** This split screen mode allows the iPad to use either camera to record footage whilst still being able to read the script.
>
> *This app is also very useful for book reviews, weather reports or poetry readings.*

6. Once the audio description, text and photographs have been inserted, discuss with the children how they could organise the museum in the classroom. For further extension work, they could create **QR codes** as an introduction to the museum, so that the *public* (invited parents, grandparents and other adults) know how to navigate around the **Smart Digital Museum**.

☁ Collaborative books

Collaborative books are a great way of joining books together or making collections of books. For example:

• Each group can produce a collated book based on a theme from the class topic. For example, *Health and Hygiene* or *Diet and Exercise* for a Year 5 Healthy Lifestyle topic.
• Produce study guides for a topic or Year 6 revision. Each group chooses a topic and writes the week's top tips or collect the learning as you go throughout the week and share the examples in one book.
• Using the teacher's iPad, set up a book for each child or if children have access to their own iPad they create their own *What I'm most proud of this ... topic/term/year* books. This is a useful, different and creative way for the children to reflect on their learning.

✑ Mash it up!

One of the advantages of Book Creator is that you can work across separate books – this even applies to books created on separate iPads, which can then be amalgamated into one larger book when you are ready or have finished the topic. The process rests on creating a final book or selecting one that has already been created and then importing the pages of the other books to the end of this final book.

You need to remember before you start that you can only combine books that have the same layout as the current book (e.g., portrait, square or landscape).

Combining pages

1. Load up the app so you can see all your books on the My Books screen.
2. Select the book you want to be the final book and will add the other pages to.
3. Press the '+' and choose 'Combine books'.
4. A menu will appear together with an image of the book. Select the book you want to combine and press 'Copy'. This will add all of the book's pages to the end of your final book. A 'Copying pages' menu will appear with a tick of when this is complete.

Repeat this action as many times as you would like, until all the books are combined.

⊗ Photo Artbooks

Creating an Artbook is a quick, easy and simple way of using Book Creator. Images can be inserted either by taking an image using the camera or by accessing the photographs already stored in the 'camera roll'. Some examples of Artbooks:

- A book to display the children's artwork. The completed book can be exported as a PDF and then embedded on the school website.
- A tour of the school at the beginning of the year for new pupils.
- Life around the world. Each group finds photographs from different areas around the world around the themes of food, animals, places to visit, culture, currency used.
- Individual family trees. This project could be transformed into a writing activity where the children could use the text tool to write facts next to the photograph.

- Explaining how to take part in an outdoor education experience or as a record of one. For example, an Artbook of some of the 50 things children need to experience before the age of 11 (this website has some further tips: www.50things.org.uk/activity-list.aspx).
- A special school event such as the end of term production. Children who are not involved or part of the media team/school's digital leaders team could take photographs of the production as a record of the experience.

To make an Artbook

1. Create a new book.
2. Use the camera app and take the selected photographs. Video can also be imported into Book Creator and is compressed on entry (*note: this will also increase the final size of the file*).
3. Press the add item '+' sign and select 'Camera'. Press the shutter button to take the photograph. An option will be displayed once the photograph is taken to either retake the photograph or use it in the book. Select '**Use**' if you are happy, and the image will fill the screen. It is worth noting that there are no crop or image editing options within Book Creator. However, a copy of the image is placed in the camera roll whereby you can press the 'Edit' option in the top right-hand corner to crop/change the colour effect/resize/rotate the image.
4. Create a front cover for your photobook.

Pages can be reordered if required. (See the next box.)

Reordering pages

1. In the top left-hand corner next to the 'My books' option is an option called '**Pages**'. This will bring up all the pages within your book.

2. Press the 'Edit' option in the top right hand corner. The pages will jiggle. Hold your finger on the page you wish to move and move it across the other pages. The other pages will then move out of the way. Release your finger when in the correct place.

3. By pressing once on a page, a menu will appear. This will allow you to copy, insert, delete and share the image with other apps installed on the iPad.

4. When you have finished, press 'Done' and then press on the page to return to the main Book Creator view.

☁ Create a dual language book

Create dual language texts for children by translating favourite stories, or encouraging parents to share stories that celebrate their cultural heritage. Invite bilingual speakers from the school community or local education authority to read the text in the representative home language.

Create a book in the usual way and make use of the '**Add image**' function to make the book as visually appealing as possible. You might start with a book for new arrivals called 'Welcome to our school'. Using the '**General**' tab, you can add a new keyboard and select this to create the text. If the language uses different characters, when you load the program next time, press and hold the globe next to the 123 numbers option in the bottom left-hand corner and the various installed keyboards can be activated.

Alternatively, text can be translated as a starting point using apps such as iTranslate (https://itunes.apple.com/gb/app/itranslate-free-translator/id288113403?mt=8) or simply Google Translator (https://translate.google.pt/?ie=UTF-8&hl=en&client=tw-ob#auto/en/).

☁ Non-fiction books

Non-fiction books are easy to create in Book Creator. For example, children can create a KS1 non-fiction book for the class home/school link toy bear; the selected child can take the bear home and photographs can be taken of the bear accompanying the child around for the week or weekend. The child and the adult can take photographs of the various activities and experiences, and draft a short piece of text before returning to school.

Ask parents to take digital photographs using their smartphone and email the images and draft writing, so the children can then use the iPad back in school to create the book page. With many parents owning smart devices, provide a link for the parents to download the app and the children can create their mini book of the time when the class toy bear came to stay. Once finished, the book can be exported through email. Whilst in book mode, click the share icon (a square box with a vertical arrow) and the epub of the final book of the bear's adventures can be emailed back to the teacher or to other family members.

There is a wide range of different types of non-fiction books which can be created using Book Creator, including:

- Non-chronological reports – for example, you can create an information leaflet about looking after guinea pigs.
- Instruction texts – you can create a fan page poster of a favourite author.
- Texts that recount information – a fun activity is to create a pictorial letter about the summer holiday.
- Argumentative texts – you could encourage children to write a short argumentative piece about why they need to spend their break indoors or outdoors, listing their key points for and against.
- Information text – you can encourage children to write the menu of a typical week's meals across a week as part of a healthy eating topic.
- Persuasive writing texts – you can ask children to write a letter to Father Christmas.

- Explanation texts – a poster explaining how the Millennium Falcon flies is a creative activity for older children.

☁ Creating comics

Similarly to the Comic Life app (Chapter 5), Book Creator has the ability to create comic strips. Load the app and select the book; underneath are another set of optional layouts in a comic book layout. All these options can be customised. Insert the panels first to build up the comic. In each panel, an image and camera icon is displayed. By using these options you can insert images from the camera roll or take a photograph and insert these directly into the comic (this makes the population easier). For further ideas and creative activities, see Chapter 5 on using the Comic Life app.

Options for creating comics

Press on the '+' sign and the 'Add item' menu will appear. This menu differs from the normal menu and is replaced with options to:

- Insert panels (these are the building blocks of the layout of the comic)
- Insert speech (this option will insert a standard looking speech bubble)
- Insert thought (this option is similar to a speech bubble but the appearance is cloudlike)
- Add text (plain text, captions and two styles of comic art text can be inserted)
- Add sound (this is the same function as the normal add sound button).

In the top right-hand corner of the menu there is a 'More' option with additional shapes and text shapes associated with comic design:

- Stickers (pre-determined comic and onomatopoeic elements which are inserted and resized in the same way images are).
- The photos, camera, pen and shapes options work in the same way as the normal Book Creator builder.

🗨 Creating a phonics/handwriting book

Insert an image of phonetic sounds or handwriting paper in order for the children to use the stylus to match the audio phoneme with its grapheme.

Start by making a new book. Stretch the image so it fills the screen. Then, press and hold a finger on the image, which will bring up the menu. Then '**Lock**' the image in place.

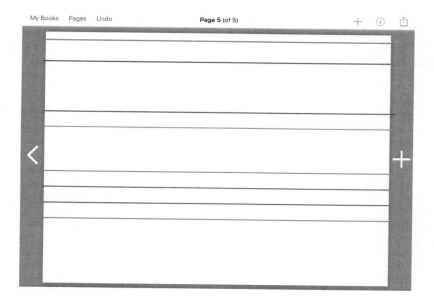

If making a handwriting book

Under **Add item** in the top right-hand corner is a **Shapes** option. Use the line and draw the correct length for the screen. Change the colour by pressing on the line and selecting the information 'i'. Finally, hold down a finger on each of the lines until a menu appears. **Lock** each of the lines in place. The children can then use a pen to practise handwriting using a stylus.

If making a phonics book

After inserting the image, record a sound file for the phoneme and drag it next to the relevant image on the page. The children can then practise specific sounds, linked to the photographs or images of objects they stand for.

⛐ Individualising e-book versions of texts

Book Creator can be used to provide support for those pupils with additional needs. The book can provide extra information about a task through the use of audio commented instructions, or children can use the books to organise their ideas before writing.

Begin a new book and add the required text by inserting an item. You can also create a worksheet for the children to support their work. This could be written instructions or questions for the children to answer. Beside each sentence, read out the sentence so there is an audio version of the sentence. Additional information can be included at the same time as reading the sentence out aloud. Once the sentence is read, drag the sound file next to the sentence. Alternatively, the children could use the sound record to record their answers to the questions you set and then write a response.

CHAPTER 16

'Great British Bake Off'

Applications

Socrative (Student/Teacher)	free	iPad/iPhone/Android
Book Creator	paid	iPad/iPhone/Android
iMovie	paid	iPad/iPhone
Comic Life	free	iPad/iPhone/Android
Explain Everything	paid	iPad/iPhone/Android
Foldify	paid	iPad/iPhone
Moldiv	free	iPad/iPhone/Android
Great British Chefs HD	free	iPad/iPhone
Kahoot	accessible via web browser	
Camera app	free	
VideoScribe	free	iPad/iPhone/Android

ACTIVITIES

There is a joy in learning to cook especially with a class of children; the food smells enrich the class environment and create a sense of anticipation before eating the final product. Popular cooking shows such as 'The Great British Bake Off' have raised awareness and provided an opportunity for discussing how cooking is viewed. Although practical in nature, apps and activities can support children in both the planning and the cooking of their final tasty creations. However, no mobile device can replace the taste test.

The task

The traditional Victoria sandwich cake and lunchbox sandwich need a revamp and they need you. You are required to help reinvent them for the 21st century before re-launching them to your parents and other adults. You will need to design everything, from the product to the marketing for your new cake or sandwich.

Let's take a poll

Design a survey to explore the cooking tastes of the class. Find out information such as:

- *Do you like cakes with fruit in them?* (Yes/No)
- *Do you like cakes with 'bits' in them such as chocolate chips or nuts?* (Short answer question)
- *Which of the following makes the best sandwich filling if you had to choose one?* Just meat, salad, fish, a mixture of meat and salad. (Multiple choice)

Ask the children to devise four key questions, similar to the examples above, but ensure that questions are asked about the class's likes of both cakes and sandwiches.

Use polling apps such as the web-based Kahoot (https://getkahoot.com) or the web and app-based Socrative (www.socrative.com) to create a poll that the children can access via their devices. You may wish for the children to work in small groups, so children can refine their questions before sharing with the rest of the class.

The voting apps work by designing the quiz (with pre-written questions) and then running the quiz. The children follow a link or enter a code to the quiz with a session in a similar way to the ClassFlow app shared in Chapter 13. Socrative and Kahoot allow the user to create quizzes with a range of questions including: multiple choice, true/false answers together with short answers. There is also the option to add images/photographs to add a visual element to the question.

Either create a teacher account for all the children to log into, or use a shared Google document or shared PrimaryPad that you, as the teacher, can generate into the shared class quiz.

 ## Cooking by numbers

Cooking programmes often break down the various and multiple stages of following a recipe. Use the camera app on your device to film the stages of how a traditional Victoria sandwich cake is made.

Film each of the separate stages; however, do not worry if, during the filming of the cooking, the clips have the children talking over them. You can edit these out later in the process.

Use iMovie to edit each clip by selecting and moving it down to the timeline. Press on the clip and trim the unwanted sections that are not required. At the bottom of the screen where the options are, press on the volume option and reduce the sound down to 0%, which will mute the unwanted talking. It is then possible to narrate a new commentary by selecting the microphone to the left of the screen and pressing 'Record'. Appropriate background music can also be added, or to create a sense of drama add a countdown. Export the finished film clip back to the camera roll.

Next, use **Book Creator** (see Chapter 15) to create a visual and multimedia version of how to cook the cake. Insert the videos one by one and illustrate the page using the pen tool and shapes. Add instructions using the text tool to complete the finished book.

As an extension task, the children can use Book Creator to design a multimedia recipe card for a World War II meal, which works particularly well using the landscape page orientation. Divide the class into groups and, working with an adult to support the process, the children can make and record how to make the chosen meal or bake. Having created the page, the children can include any facts they have gathered from their historical research or reading about wartime food.

Cooking comics

Use Comic Life (or the Book Creator with the comic templates selected) as a way of recording how to cook a recipe. Within the app, there are prepared 'How to guide' templates, which can be used as inspiration or as a scaffold support for the children. Populate the comic with photographs from the cooking process by adding speech bubbles where appropriate with helpful hints for the reader. As an extension task, host a food tasting and encourage the children to rate the success of the cooking by adding a star rating using the shape tool. The comics can then be reproduced in the school newspaper, providing an audience and purpose for writing.

 How do the experts do it?

There are a number of apps which both promote healthy eating and display food in an attractive way, for instance visit apps such as Great British Chefs Kids HD (https://itunes.apple.com/gb/app/great-british-chefs-kids-hd/id639554061?mt=8&ign-mpt=uo%3D4).

Explore the app and ask the children to consider how it sets out the various recipes. Are the photographs of the food taken as close-ups or from a distance? What is the effect of this? Why do they do this? What is the structure of a recipe? What is mentioned first and what comes after? Reflect on the key features of a chosen recipe and explain what makes it successful as a persuasive advert.

 Skills development

Use the camera tool or Explain Everything (see Chapter 7) to produce a video help-file to teach the children cooking skills (chop, blend, simmer, fold in mixture). Demonstrate each skill in turn to the children, and then using their mobile device they can film the demonstration or instruction to support their learning. This will be especially useful before the children use sharp tools on the real piece of food. Embed the videos onto a class blog that the children can refer to whilst cooking at home with their parents/caregivers, which is a useful strategy to develop home/school links.

Promoting your new cake/sandwich

Design a poster for the launch of your cake or sandwich using Moldiv. Take a photograph of the finished cake/sandwich and design a poster to capture the attention of the consumer. Reflect back on the learning from **How do the experts do it?** and explore the effectiveness of the visual advertising before looking at the various slogans which are aimed at persuading the customer to buy products.

 Produce a marketing video/explanation using VideoScribe

Explore the VideoScribe (www.videoscribe.co/anywhere) app to make a marketing video for the newly designed and advertised cake or sandwich. VideoScribe uses a technique that customises images and text, which is then dragged onto the screen to create an animation. Each element brought onto the screen creates another section of the animation timeline.

When the animation is played, each part of the image or piece of text appears, as if hand-drawn, and a real image of a human hand sketches the image/text on the screen. A large library of images is available as well as the ability to import your own. Finally, a backing track can be inserted through the music library and there is the possibility to add narration, so the children can explain the product to their consumer. Sir Ken Robinson uses this technique in his RSA Animate talk 'Changing Education Paradigms' (www.ted.com/talks/ken_robinson_changing_education_paradigms).

 Packaging your new cake/sandwich

Ask the children to use Foldify to design and make the packaging for their new cake or sandwich. As a separate drawing activity, the children can design their front cover, as well as the different design elements they wish to include on the packaging. Explore the different types of packaging that sandwiches and cakes are wrapped in and the type of nutritional information that is included.

In the app, navigate to the stamp icon (i.e. the face consisting of glasses, a nose and a moustache). From here, there are different pre-created stamps that can be dragged onto the various sides of the packaging. There is also an option to take a photograph or to import one. Ask the children to take a photograph of their front cover and drag it on to the front of the box and then stretch it out. Then, using the tools within the app, draw and photograph the different elements, in order to complete the design for their new cake/sandwich. Finally, print out the finished packaging and assemble it, before displaying in the classroom.

OTHER APPS

TocaMonster

Teacher tools

Throughout this book, we have covered some tried and tested activities of using apps with KS2 children in the classroom. A creative teacher would come up with ideas for using the apps not only for teaching purposes but also their own use.

For instance, Our Story has been used by teachers to document and share children's work and progress; a multimedia story was in this instance not created by the child but by the teacher, using the same procedure. Similarly, QR codes can be used to share video content in the classroom but also with colleagues in the school or other schools, showcasing innovative practice.

In many UK classrooms with tablets, teachers have their own device which they can take home and populate with apps of their choice. This is a good option to ensure the teacher is up to date and familiar with the latest software. If you are one of the teachers who own their own tablet or smartphone, you may be interested in creating your own digital content. The more you can create your own digital resources, the more likely your students become inspired to create their own too (and not just passively consume what others have designed for them). The Nesta Digital Makers program has some tips for how to encourage young people to create their own content with digital tools (http://www.nesta.org. uk/project/digital-makers/).

Social media apps

Twitter, Facebook, Google+ and other social media platforms where you keep in touch with your friends and colleagues are not all optimised for all devices, but opening them up on your teacher's device shouldn't be a problem. These apps can be a great way to get personalised recommendations and updates on specific issues, but be wary of the pitfalls of using social media on personal devices in school. A popular blog post listing the key dangers is here: www.teachertoolkit.me/2015/02/06/social-media-failure-from-the-classroom-by-digitalsisters/.

Discussing the use of social media networks with your students is a great way of becoming part of their 'digital world' and teaching some key digital literacy skills around security, privacy and ethics.

BLOGGING

The nine key reasons for why teachers should blog are, according to Tsisana Palmer, Intensive English Program Instructor and a popular teacher blogger, the following: teachers who blog can share, reflect, publish, improve their reading skills, serve others, lead their own PD, become a digital citizen, be ahead of their students, showcase student work. If you would like to join the lively teacher blogging community, you can comment on others' posts or start a blog of your own. If you would like to start your teaching blog on a free site, we recommend WordPress and the WordPress app, which is compatible with iPad and free. The app has a nice interface, affording an easy way to respond to your followers' comments, edit post and view at a glance your stats (how many times has a blog been read).

Some popular teacher blogging sites

There are thousands of teachers' blogs and you probably have your favourite ones already. These are the top three blogging sites we love:

- The Behaviour Guru by Tom Bennett, which inspired his book *The Behaviour Guru: Behaviour Management Solutions for Teachers*. Tom also regularly writes for *TES* on a variety of topics: http://behaviourguru.blogspot.pt/
- Described as the most influential blog on education in the UK, with a set of engaging techniques for effective teaching, it is written by a deputy headteacher who has more than 120k followers on Twitter: see the @TeacherToolkit: www.teachertoolkit.me/
- Agility-Teaching Toolkit, written by several teachers and thus offering greater variety of content, contains some short tips and tested techniques: www.cheneyagilitytoolkit.blogspot.co.uk/

Our three favourite blogging sites specifically focused on educational technology (including apps) are:

- www.whiteboardblog.co.uk/
- http://edtechteacher.org/apps/#Begin
- http://ictevangelist.com/

AUDIOBOOKS

Audiobooks have several benefits for children as well as the teacher. Rather than just taking off the burden of having to read aloud, audiobooks can be an exciting way of nurturing readers' identities and long-term pleasure for reading. To move beyond tokenistic use, you can use audiobooks to portray the various characters in a book and illustrate an artistic interpretation of a text. Reflecting on the audio-recording quality (voice choice, pitch, sound effects) will inspire students' own read-alouds. Tablets can be used for 'audiobooks boots'; all you need is to download some audiobooks (or use a strong internet connection to stream them) and have a set of headphones. To download free audiobooks, check out Openculture (www.openculture.com/freeaudiobooks) which offers a comprehensive list of 700 free fiction and literature audiobooks. Place the tablets with downloaded books in a quiet corner in the classroom and encourage children to go and listen to stories at break or playtime.

Create your own audiobooks

Professionally made audiobooks are great but what about making your own? To create your own audiobook, you can use an audio-recording app (see Chapter 6 for details) and add some music or simple sounds to accompany the reading. Children will appreciate seeing that stories are not just about reading fluency but also aesthetic qualities (which include sound effects). Sharing your own audiobooks with the class can be extended to home and encouraging the children to create their own audiobooks, perhaps together with family members for more fun. Co-created audiobooks are a fantastic way to celebrate literature and the spoken word.

PODCASTS AND VODCASTS

A podcast is an audio recording (or a series of audio recordings) shared online. A vodcast is a video podcast, that is a video broadcast over the internet. However, a podcast is not just a simple audio file uploaded online (and a vodcast is not just a video shared on YouTube). The main difference is that it is made available using a subscription 'feed' (e.g., RSS, Really Simple Syndication) which users subscribe to and set their devices to automatically download new content from. You might be familiar with various podcast channels offered by major radio channels (e.g., www.bbc.co.uk/podcasts) which you can subscribe to and listen to on your tablet. If you have an iPad, then you would subscribe and play a podcast via iTunes, for tablets it's Windows Media Player. For videocasts, you will need an MP3 video player, automatically available with most tablets and iPads.

Create your own podcasts and vodcasts

You can use podcasts and vodcasts to introduce professional voices and experts into the classroom and provide extra information or a new angle on a topic. Creating your own podcast/vodcast does take some time though.

To create a **podcast**, you need a microphone and an audio-recording app. To ensure high-quality recording, use an external microphone or a sound-proof (or very quiet) room. It's very rare to record a podcast at the first go, without the need for editing. This is why podcasting takes time! Audacity (http://audacityteam.org/) is a free audio-recording software which can be downloaded on your desktop PC, and free audio editing apps exist for iPad and tablets (e.g., the Hokusai Audio editor for iPads or WavePad for tablets). Save the finished audio recording as an MP3 file and upload it to iTunes (if you are an iPad user) or any of the popular educational podcast sites; our favourite one is the Education Podcast Network for and by teachers: www.edupodcastnetwork.com/.

To create a **vodcast**, you will need to use a camera, such as the one embedded in the tablet or in your smartphone. To edit your video file, you can use the traditional, free video-editing software available for desktop PCs and laptops (e.g., Windows Movie Maker or iMovie for Macs) or video-editing apps (e.g., iMovie for iPads is a paid app with similar interface to that of iMovie on a Mac and Powerdirector is a popular video-editing app for tablets). A good vodcast is usually about 3–5 minutes long and you can find many examples of popular, teacher-created vodcasts at: www.schooltube.com/.

SHARING FILES

If you use and produce digital content, you will need to have a sharing and synchronising mechanism in place. Synchronisation is about ensuring that the content you have for example on your smartphone is also available on your desktop PC. Sharing is about sending your files to the devices of your students, their parents or your colleagues.

Dropbox is the most popular service for synchronising files (video, audio, texts or pictures) across your own device and sharing them with others. You can download Dropbox on your computer or as an app on your iPad or tablet. The app works across any devices, which means that what you store on one device will be automatically synchronised with your other device, and made available to you as soon as you log in to your password-protected account. There is no restriction on the type of files (.pdf, .doc, .dox or .jpg and .mov are all fine). The service is, however, a third-party service, so you can never be sure that your files are 100% secure. Although Dropbox Ltd. guarantees that their cloud service applies strict security policies, it has been criticised in the past for several incidents of security and privacy breaches.

Another similar and free service (but carrying the same security risks) is Google Drive which offers slightly more storage (15 GB free while Dropbox offers 2GB free). Paid premium services offer more storage and more flexibility of sharing. We do not recommend these sharing services for strictly confidential documents. However, for sharing content you have permissions for, Dropbox and Google Drive are the most straightforward choices.

CUSTOMISING TEACHING CONTENT AND MANAGING DEVICES

Creating your own digital content implies the need for sharing it with students. You can share your audiobooks, podcasts or vodcasts via the internet and ask the children to download them on their individual devices. Alternatively, you can populate the devices using AirDrop or another file-sharing service. These techniques, however, take time and effort. An easy and secure way of sharing content across many or groups of devices is offered by the so-called device-management apps and services. These allow you to customise the class content and easily share and synchronise it across devices. The most popular platforms offering this service for schools are ClassFlow, AirWatch for Education and Nearpod. These apps and services are not free and the pricing options depend on the school's structure, number of devices subscribed to the service and others. The advantage of the system is that it supports customisation on the device level, that is you can create groups and specify the content for each individual group. For example, a group of students can be assigned photographs from World War II and a suite of apps relevant for this topic, while another group of students can be working on a parallel project. You can also send different content to different students (if there is a tablet per student in the classroom). The individualisation options are particularly useful for self-paced assessments, with questions adjusted to different levels of difficulty. The results can be aggregated by self-defined groups (at the classroom, school or LA level).

The systems are platform agnostic which means that you can populate the tablet devices from any other tablet or desktop PC; use any file format, including PDF and jpg images and any browser, including Google Chrome or Safari.

These systems greatly save cost and allow teachers to better monitor and facilitate tablet work, respecting their preferences and security concerns.